Praise for J

"This little book presents a clear, actionable wisdom you can use throughout life to help understand and transform your relationships."
—**Andy Andrews, *New York Times* Bestselling Author of *The Traveler's Gift* and *The Noticer***

"We spend many years on the 'three R's'... but precious little time on the fourth, which is probably most important: relationships. Susie Miller gets to the heart of what makes relationships thrive in all the messiness and stress of life. This book is a treasure that you can read in a couple hours but that will benefit you for the rest of your life."
—**Brian D. McLaren, Author/Speaker/Theologian/Global Networker, www.brianmclaren.net**

"Every once in a while a fresh voice arrives on the scene that cuts through the jargon and meets us right where we are. Susie Miller is exactly that! Her sage advice and authentic, upbeat style had me hooked from page one. *Listen, Learn, Love* is for everyone who longs for those deep, abiding relationships that make life meaningful."
—**Ann Vertel, Ph.D., Psychologist, www.AnnVertel.com**

"This is *not* another pop psychology book that gathers dust on your bookshelf. Susie Miller has written a passionate, engaging workbook that grabs you from the first page to the last. *Listen, Learn, Love* breaks the rules by giving you simple strategies that can help everyone communicate better, listen better, and rebuild your relationships no matter how broken they seem to be. Get a pen and a highlighter, and mark up these pages. This is the relationship workbook you didn't know existed. I highly recommend Susie's game-changing work."
—**Brad Szollose, Global Business Adviser/Award-winning author of *Liquid Leadership: From Woodstock to Wikipedia***

"In this meaning-filled, life-encouraging book, Susie Miller invites us all (male or female) to life lived to the fullest, no matter where on the planet we live, no matter our age. This phrase caught my full attention in her introduction: simple, elegant, and effective. That sets the tone, the direction, the focus for what you will encounter. I will read this again, and then again, as life unfolds across the years. Your life, my life, will be more whole and engaged for reading and living out its deeply valued themes. I trust the wisdom of these pages because I personally know Susie and know that she lives what she writes."
—Wes Roberts, Founder/CCO/Master Mentor Leadership Design Group, www.leadershipdesigngroup.com

"Whether it's a challenging coworker or a tricky teen, when relationships are strained, so are we. Susie brings a wealth of insight and inspiration to all of these situations in a wonderfully conversational way, helping you apply the principles in a practical way. She enables us to take our relationships to a REALational level, so they're more honest, more rewarding, and more fruitful, which in turn allows us to make the world a better place! Reading *Listen, Learn, Love* is like listening to a trusted friend talking over a cup of coffee; don't miss this wonderful book."
—Jenny Flintoft, Coach/Speaker/Consultant, www.jennyflintoft.com

"Relationships are far more art than science. Far more subtlety than strategy. Having committed herself to the art of subtlety for over 20 years, Susie Miller has crafted a wonderfully practical guide to developing skills that lead to scientifically sound relationships. Pulling from personal experience, ancient wisdom, and even pop culture, she offers actionable insights for developing deep, satisfying relationships in a hurry. Sounds counterintuitive, but the principles of *Listen, Learn, Love* are actually profoundly simple."
—Zach Brittle, LMHC, Certified Gottman Institute Therapist, www.zachbrittle.com

"In *Listen, Learn, Love*, Susie Miller offers a rich unfolding of the fundamental importance of whole and healthy relationships that speak to our deepest human longings. But further, she graciously, with authenticity and transparency, offers profoundly simple but transforming guidance on how to build, heal, and restore relationships in practical but profound insights that will serve anyone who reads this book. As someone who had been committed to relational ministry for forty years, reading this wonderful book offered me some delightful disciplines that offered guidance and growth in my own journey of friendship!"
—**Dr. Lee Corder, Senior Vice-President,**
Young Life International

"How many of us take the intimate relationships of our lives for granted? We often lack the tools to make even our most familial connections work. In her book, Susie Miller unpacks a common sense practicum that is simple, yet profound. She shows how to invest in your relationships to unlock their deepest potential. *Listen, Love, Learn* decodes the process in an entertaining and informative way. You owe it to those around you to learn this stuff!"
—**Glenn Steers, International Relationship Manager,**
Adventures in Missions

"*Listen, Learn, Love*! Sounds simple, right? Those three simple words can truly improve your relationship, and Susie does a wonderful job sharing exactly how it can improve your relationship in 30 days! Don't be deceived by the title or size of this book, because it is truly a goldmine and one everyone should have in their own personal library. Thanks, Susie!"
—**Dr. Daisy Sutherland, Speaker/Author of** *Dr. Mommy*
Life Lessons & Letting Go of Supermom/**Founder/CEO of**
WholisticFitLiving.com

"In Susie Miller's new book you quickly discover why improved relationships are essential to a better life. Her career and stories make this book not only relevant, but required reading. As I perused the pages of the manuscript I kept seeing glimpses of my own life and relationships—some good, some not so good—flash before my eyes. When you connect at that level, you have accomplished something special. This book and the wisdom contained within it will not only save countless relationships, but it will also help grow and blossom many new ones. A great book we can all use and apply each day!"
—**Tony Rubleski, Bestselling Author & Consultant, MindCaptureGroup.com**

"*Listen, Learn, Love* is a remarkably practical guide to mending and building on long-lasting relationships. Miller is refreshingly down to earth in her approach, which greatly appeals to me. She offers something that every single relationship can benefit from, and for that I am grateful."
—**Dr. Michele Summers Colon, DPM, MS, www.drmichele.com**

"Since the beginning of time the world has grown because of relationships. Healthy, vibrant, giving relationships are at the heart of life and the foundation to success. This is not just a book for your library but also a necessary tool for living life to the fullest. This book is a treasure with loads of practical advice condensed into a quick read and actionable steps to transform your relationships. When we are born, the doctor should slap our behind and hand us this book."
—**Tim Davis, Speaker/John Maxwell Certified Coach/Author of *The Marketing Evangelist*, themarketingevangelist.com**

"As a social marketing stylist, I know that social media 'caught on' because people want to be connected. They want to be acknowledged. However, for many that is easy to do online. But

offline? That is a different story. Author Susie Miller, in her book *Listen, Learn, Love…* takes relationship building to exciting new levels. In the opening pages… she makes the reader warmly comfortable with a sense that she really is on our side and gives us a sense that we can certainly master this. Miller takes the time in her writing to make sure the reader understands the concepts by delivering personal stories and anecdotes and personal lessons that the reader can easily relate to. I also liked her invitation to take notes throughout the book! You won't feel alone in your yearning for love and stronger life relationships after reading this book. Her guide makes living a life with full and complete loving relationships with family, friends, and significant others a completely possible one!"
—Jennifer Abernethy, 2x National Author/Digital Strategist/Entrepreneur, www.sociallydelivered.com

"I've read hundreds of books in the personal development industry but this one was different. *Listen, Learn, Love* had me wanting more, page after page. I couldn't put it down and found myself wanting to get to the next page and the next chapter, and I immediately wanted to start reading it all over again. Susie Miller has proven in this book that any relationship can be repaired or strengthened, and she shows you how. From the bedroom to the boardroom, be it family, friends, peers or clients, *Listen, Learn, Love* will teach you step-by-step how to have better relationships in *all* areas of your life. The real-life stories, Susie's own personal stories, and the action steps she provides have together created a beautiful masterpiece—a book that every person on the planet who is breathing needs to read—not once, but over and over again as a reminder of the difference that strengthening your relationships can have on your life."
—Susan Brady, Coach/Speaker/Trainer, www.Susan-Brady.com

"Relationships are vital to meaningful existence, for it is in the context of understanding and serving one another that we discover God. *Listen, Learn, Love* journals Susie's practical wisdom from years of dedicated practice in helping clients develop significant relationships with each other to help readers love others better. A worthwhile endeavor, indeed."
—**Andrew Greer, #1-Selling Singer-Songwriter/Author of** *Transcending Mysteries: Who Is God, and What Does He Want from Us?*

"*Listen, Learn, Love* is a book that will touch the hearts of Millennials and Baby Boomers alike, those who are single, those who are married, and those who just want to be a better person. Susie Miller walks her readers through a journey in this book. You'll be brought to tears as you imagine yourself in some of her examples, and you'll laugh at the stories she shares. Simply put, this book will remind you of the most important part of life: your relationships."
—**Jessica Rhodes, Founder, Interview Connections, InterviewConnections.com**

"I'm often asked to review business books, so when my friend Susie Miller asked me to review her new book about relationships, I knew I was in uncharted territory! To my great surprise and delight, I found myself totally enjoying her book and real-world practical advice! In life, what matters most are relationships. And whether you're an entrepreneur, married to one, or simply in a relationship that is 'less than you would like'—I encourage you to read this book. What I liked most about *Listen, Learn, Love* is the simple yet effective suggestions Susie offers to take your relationships to a higher, more rewarding level. If you feel you 'need' this book—get it now. If you feel you do not need this book, you do—Get it now. You'll be glad you did!"
—**Jim Palmer, Dream Business Coach/ Author/Speaker, www.GetJimPalmer.com**

"In this messy world we live in that promotes using violence, insults, and badmouthing our loved ones, this book is exactly what is needed to break the messiness of our relationships and turn them into connections we truly treasure and enjoy every day. Susie has a beautiful way of inviting readers to understand how possible it is to have relationships they enjoy. I highly recommend this book for those who are just starting a new relationship and want to build skills from the foundation of the relationship and for those, like me, who've been married for 10+ years and can use these skills to enhance the communication between each other."
—**Maruxa Murphy, Author/Coach/Founder of InspireAwesome.com**

"When we find ourselves stuck in a relational rut, the reason is often because we tend to view other people as extensions of our own lives, rather than seeing them as having stories of their own. What if we could learn how to be present—really present—with the people we know and love? What would it be like if we could see others in the context of their own stories? Susie's book is tremendously helpful in the process of getting to know others as those who have their own stories. You will find her techniques toward listening, learning, and loving to be invaluable help in entering the lives of others in meaningful ways."
—**Dr. Liam Atchison, Vice-President for U.S. Relations, Global Scholars**

"In her book, *Listen, Learn, Love*, Susie Miller offers wonderful insights to the essentials of healthy relationships. They are what I call the simple but profound principles when practiced consistently. For you, and those special people in your life, there could be no better gift."
— **Michael Ellison, Trivita Founder and CEO**

"*Listen, Learn, Love* is an essential guide to creating and sustaining better relationships. It is overflowing with practical tips that will work with your spouse, children, friends, and colleagues. Susie Miller's message is original, insightful, and immensely helpful."
—**Sheree Keys, #1 Bestselling Author/CEO of Smart Women's Institute, Mom of Four, www.ShereeKeys.com**

"*Listen, Learn, Love* should be an 'Operational Handbook' for all couples, or anyone wanting to go beyond simply good relationships and experience the true joy of a deep, satisfying relationship. Susie's tools are simple to understand, and easy to implement, but loaded with the power to change any relationship for the better!"
—**Julie Weaver, National Sales Director, Mary Kay, Inc.**

"Thank you, Susie Miller, for this simple yet profound book. *Listen, Learn, Love* shares valuable tools, tips, and techniques that I can use instantly to help improve my relationships. It is truly when we listen that we can learn more about love. And love makes all relationships better!"
—**Diane Cunningham, Founder and President, National Association of Christian Women Entrepreneurs, www.nacwe.org**

Listen, Learn, Love

Listen, Learn, Love

How to Dramatically
Improve Your Relationships
in 30 Days or Less!

Susie Albert Miller, MA, MDiv

Listen, Learn, Love © 2015 Susie Albert Miller

All rights reserved. No part of this book may be reproduced in any form or by any means—electronic, mechanical, photocopying, scanning, or otherwise—without permission in writing from the publisher, except by a reviewer who may quote brief passages in a review. For information on licensing or special sales, please email Dunham Books at info@dunhamgroupinc.com

This book is intended to provide accurate information with regards to the subject matter covered. However, the Author and the Publisher accept no responsibility for inaccuracies or omissions, and the Author and Publisher specifically disclaim any liability, loss, or risk, whether personal, financial, or otherwise, that is incurred as a consequence, directly or indirectly, from the use and/or application of any of the contents of this book.

Library of Congress Control Number: 2015931332
Trade Paperback ISBN: 978-1-939447-74-6
Ebook ISBN: 978-1-939447-85-2

Cover design by Caye Howe, Firefly Graphics

Printed in the United States of America

For

John, Kate, Emily and Zack,

God's canvas for teaching me about the depth of His love,

and the messy, yet glorious art of relationships.

Contents

"Lots of people want to ride with you in the limo,
but what you want is someone who will
take the bus with you
when the limo breaks down."
—Oprah Winfrey

Foreword

Relationships. It's a weighty word, isn't it? It's heavy with our preconceived notions and meanings we've derived from our own hopes and history.

In a world where it is so easy to "friend and unfriend"— perhaps we've lost sight of what a true relationship is and how to nurture and grow that. After all, we can simply change our "relationship status" with the click of a button, right? Our emotions of the moment and our feelings at the time dictate the relationships that we are willing to declare. Wow.

The marketplace is ripe with books, manuals, and magazine articles on "How To's" ranging from *Finding Your Perfect Mate* to *Dumping Your Toxic Pals*. Everywhere you turn there are reports of fairy tales and epic fails. But who is dealing with the messy middle? Who is willing to delve into the humdrum of daily life and help us know that it can also be spectacular?

Susie Miller is doing just that with an inspiring yet practical guide that covers the essentials everyone needs to know. And she's not shaking her fist, stomping her foot, and demanding that you "Speak Up! Be Heard! Be Loved Like You Deserve!" Instead, with rich authenticity and honesty, she gently reminds us that the real treasure can be found when you *Listen, Learn, Love.*

I'll be the first to admit that I have no license, certification, or degree in people or relationships. I've got my own share of drama and trauma, just like you!

But perhaps what I've learned as a U.S. Coast Guard Officer's kid, a preacher's daughter (in Dad's second career) and now as a business speaker and consultant, is that when you mine relationships for gold… there is platinum to be found. There is joy in the thread of human connection.

Is it work? Heck, yeah! Is it worth it? You better believe it!

Susie tackles all of this, and more… and not in rhetorical, hand-slapping or preachy ways, but in transformational ways like you've never imagined.

Read this. Heed this. Share this. Then watch and see what happens!

—Carrie Wilkerson

Author of *The Barefoot Executive*
CarrieWilkerson.com

A Note from the Author

"Hearts will never be practical,
until they are made unbreakable."
—*Wizard of Oz*

If you are sitting in tense silence at the dinner table, tired of going to bed angry, worn out from arguing with your kids, feeling lonely in your friendships, distant from your parents and siblings, frustrated with your work relationships... or if you simply want more from your relationships, this little book can help!

We don't grow up hoping our life and relationships will be average. We dream of connection, deep friendships, rich family time, and thriving, productive work relationships. Life happens; tension, difficulties, and disappointments flood our relationships and we muddle through. Without thinking, we try not to feel or acknowledge that most of our relationships are more gray-toned and draining than sun-filled and satisfying. We wonder what happened... but we are often too busy, or overwhelmed, or feel ill equipped to make changes.

If we're honest, really honest... we know our hearts want more. We watch chick flicks—yes, even guys sometimes—with misty eyes and longing. We cheer for the good guy, hoping he gets the girl and they actually do live happily ever after. Sometimes we reminisce about our buddies on the football team and the good old days of high school. We read success stories of business partnerships or winning collaborations and imagine ourselves in these settings. With jealousy and longing, we read blogs and Facebook posts of families making memories and sharing life—wishing ours could do the same.

Let's admit it: You and I want more from our relationships, but we are hesitant to believe it's possible, let alone doable!

What if you could improve each of your relationships without a major overhaul or personality transplant? What if learning and practicing a few skills could make a significant difference? What if your childhood hopes about relationships could actually be realized?! I imagine these few "what ifs" prompted you to pick up this book, and I'm so glad you did. Because your relationships can improve and become enjoyable and satisfying; it is not only possible—but also attainable—using the skills in this book. Countless people have used them in all types of relationships and have had great success, even if they were the only person applying them. Relationships are tricky that way... When one person makes an effort, things begin to change!

Relationships fascinate me. I have studied them and worked in the field of psychology—coaching, equipping, and helping people develop better relationships—for more than 20 years professionally and, as long as I can remember, personally. I was the mediator, the go-between, the *let me see if I can help you understand what she meant* go-to girl in my family and friendships.

I never expected my life's work would be helping people create better relationships with themselves, God, and others. Maybe I was naïve. A number of years ago, at the end of one of my seminars on "Trusting God through Seasons of Struggle and Sorrow," a woman approached me and asked how I chose the field of counseling. I hesitated before answering her: "Most people choose this field because somewhere in their story they have experienced trauma, struggle, sorrow, or loss, and someone helped them through it… and they want to do the same for others. That is true for me, so I guess you could say it chose me!"

God has used the experiences, struggles, and difficulties as well as the joys, blessings, and—most of all—the people in my life to grow me, teach me, and train me about relationships. At times my journey was confusing, unsettling, and incredibly painful. But, I firmly believe that God is good—Life and relationships can be rich and rewarding even in the midst of difficult times. I know this truth from personal experience, and I long to share it with as many people as possible. After years in private practice as a Marriage and Family Therapist,

I became a Marriage and Relationship Coach so I could reach more people, offering hope and specific tools to transform their relationships and lives. No matter where you are in life, there is always hope! I promise.

Thank you for picking up this book. Thank you for trusting me to walk with you into the most significant part of your life—the people you share it with. I applaud your willingness to risk, grow, change, and invest in your relationships. I have been where you are... wondering if a relationship will make it, staring at the slammed door, dreading the tension-filled work environment. Wondering *what is wrong with me? Why is this so hard?* Or being mad at *them* for being such *jerks*.

Some days I am still there—in the midst of messy, complicated relationships—wanting more, making mistakes, and sometimes tempted to give up. Writing this book was risky because the people in my life live the ups and downs of being in relationship with me. They know I don't always apply what I teach. They will read these words and see my shortcomings. While they enjoy the blessings of our relationship, they also bear the brunt of my failures.

Maybe that is what qualifies me to write this book. All of my degrees, training, and work experience aside, my own relationships are my greatest teacher. I work hard to create authentic and strong ones, but I too am a work in progress. I'll share personal stories of my successes and failures, as I am learning alongside you. Enjoyable and thriving relationships are possible—not always easy, but worth the effort.

Every relationship has tough spots, tension, silence, or loud moments. If someone tells you otherwise, they are probably not being honest. People who enjoy healthy, thriving, and satisfying relationships have learned to navigate through difficult times with authenticity, perspective, and skills. You can too!

Relationships can get better. You can grow and change; life can be different. While this book doesn't specifically focus on personal growth or developing a deeper faith, I do have programs and resources that do, so don't walk alone if you are struggling. Grab a cup of coffee, friend me on Facebook for some encouragement and inspiration, or go to my blog (susiemiller.com) and have a virtual chat with me. Explore the resources on my website; download some free ones or sign up for a seminar or coaching program. Remember, we are just one choice away from making a change in our life.

In the meantime, read on and commit to working on improving your relationships. Change and growth happen by taking one step, then another—over and over again. Relationships are the stuff of life and worth the energy and time investment to make them great. In the end… they are all that really matter.

Chapter 1

You Don't Have to Settle for *Less Than*

"The best and most beautiful things in the world
cannot be seen or even touched—
they must be felt with the heart."
—*Helen Keller*

Are you tired of struggling in your relationships? Do you want to connect with your spouse, kids, family, friends, and/or coworkers but aren't sure how to move from silence or tension to conversations and connections that develop into deeper relationships?

Can you remember the last time your spouse smiled at the end of a conversation and said, "Thanks for listening… for really understanding what I am trying to say"?

Are you dizzy from your teen rolling their eyes at you and loudly sighing multiple times in the course of a discussion?

When your coworker shared an idea to tweak your process or broached a business issue with you, was your response, "Wow, you really get it! Thanks for bringing that up; I am looking forward to working on this with you"?

Are you avoiding having the difficult discussion with your siblings and aging parents about their future plans because you anticipate the conversation deteriorating into a tense squabble reminiscent of your growing-up years?

Well…

- *What if* you could dramatically change the way your conversations go?
- *What if* you could engage in difficult discussions and they actually went well?
- *What if* your conversations with your spouse led to deeper intimacy rather than distance?
- *What if* talks with your kids brought you closer together, if they felt like you understood them and began to share more openly?
- *What if* your work relationships felt more like partnerships than transactions because the conversations and collaborations surrounding your work together were seamless?

Does this sound too good to be true?

It's not!

Three Skills for Creating Better Relationships

The words *Listen, Learn, Love* don't necessarily sound like revolutionary skills. In fact, they seem pretty basic. However, I have found some simple, elegant, and effective ways to teach and practice these skills that can actually improve relationships quickly.

- **Simple:** because they are small tweaks to basic and foundational skills.
- **Elegant:** because they are nuanced, subtle, and timeless, yet can have a huge impact. Like a little black dress that steals the show on the red carpet, elegance goes a long way.
- **Effective:** because they are foolproof and work!

They are the fundamentals in all my work as a relationship and marriage coach.

Skill #1: Listen. Sounds simple and rather like a no-brainer, but you would be surprised at how much we don't really listen to one another. Oh, we hear the words people speak, but their message often gets lost for a number of reasons. We will explore those reasons and how to effectively use this skill. *Listening* can make almost any relationship better fast!

Skill #2: Learn Them. Do you really know the people in your relationships, not just on a surface level, but their hopes, dreams, fears, and stories? We will unpack how *Learning Them* can enhance and improve your relationships in rapid and surprising ways.

Skill #3: Love Well. Relationships—great relationships— are built on a foundation of giving, of putting the other person and their needs first. We will explore what it means to *Love Well* and how to practice it in your relationships to achieve dramatic results quickly.

When you read the book title, did you wonder if relationships could dramatically improve in 30 days or less?

It may seem like an outrageous claim, but in my experience you really can get rapid results. Many people who have applied these skills enjoyed improvements within 30 days, in some as soon as 24 hours!

So, once you start using the skills, watch for changes in your relationships and see if it works. Sure... we live in an instant-gratification society, but creating better relationships in 24 hours to 30 days isn't too shabby!

Now, as we begin this journey, you'll get to know a little about me in the process. And one of the things that's important for you to know is I love art. I love color, texture, and creating environments that express good thoughts and feelings. My home is filled with art and images that remind me of meaningful moments, important ideas, and, of course, treasured relationships.

As I was thinking about *Listen, Learn, Love*, I realized that there were ways that I could "anchor" these thoughts with symbols: *Listen* (as I kid, I remember trying to listen to the ocean with a conch shell), *Learn* (as I've gotten older I realize that glasses make the world clearer!) and *Love* (the universal symbol to remind us of our hearts).

The three symbols on the cover help me remember not only each individual skill, but the nuances of it as well.

I remember walking on the beach when I was younger and my mom handing me a conch shell. She told me hold it up to my ear, be very still, and listen so I could hear the ocean. I remember being skeptical; how could a simple shell hold the majestic sound of waves and water? Pensively holding it to my ear, I remember being delighted with the ocean sounds caught deep inside. Carrying it home on my lap, I would periodically pick it up and listen again, just to be sure the ocean was still there and I didn't miss anything.

Once I got home, I would return to my conch shell, holding it to my ear, and be transported back to the sunny and restful days in the sand. *Listening* is like that. A wealth of information, beauty, and connection comes when we pause and pay attention. When we learn to really listen, we discover things we never knew, information and understanding we can return to time and again to deepen our connection and improve our relationships.

Consistent with my love of art, I have numerous pairs of "artsy" glasses. I now have three different kinds of glasses, one for distance, one for reading, and a third pair called "computer distance" glasses, somewhere between the strength of the first two pairs. Juggling them is a comedy act and invariably I have a pair perched on my head, while simultaneously trying to find them. My eyesight isn't terrible and I can get away without wearing them, but I miss the finer details when I do. And I have to make the font on my iPhone or Kindle extra-large to read it without the use of reading glasses. I don't particularly like glasses so I squint and struggle to see when I am too vain to wear them. *Learning* is a bit like that. It isn't always easy and comfortable. It requires us to set aside our assumptions and pay attention to what is happening below the surface. All of us need to check our vision and be attuned to information obscured by masks or the polish we all wear to present the "me" we think people want to see.

As we learn about people, we often need new lenses to see the real people behind the façades and first impressions, as well as our assumptions about others. Glennon Doyle Melton, author of *Carry On, Warrior: The Power of Embracing Your Messy, Beautiful Life,* calls this "wearing *perspectacles*"—a brilliant word and profoundly clear way to understand this concept. We all need "*perspectacles*" to see beyond the obvious, set aside our preconceived notions, look beneath the surface, and learn about one another in order to create deeper levels of connection.

Hearts are funny things. Like the word "love," they have been overused and cheapened, yet they still signify the deepest part of us. Look around at all the ways we use and misuse hearts: "you have my whole heart for my whole life," "I heart U", dotting the letter "i" with a heart. We talk about being brokenhearted, hard-hearted, full-hearted, wholehearted... Our hearts are essential to life, literally and figuratively. Learning to *Love Well*, being vulnerable, authentic, connected, and sacrificial comes from our heart as much as our mind. As a coach and therapist, one of the first things I do is teach the principles of *Listen, Learn, Love.* Once people begin applying these skills, they can't wait to tell me about the meaningful conversations, increased intimacy, and deeper connections they enjoy with the people in their lives. They sometimes think I am a magician or a miracle worker! I assure them: It is *their* efforts to learn and use these skills that are responsible for the positive changes in their relationship. Now you can create this same type of "relationship magic" by learning and practicing them as well.

A Virtual Personal Chat

Imagine we are sitting in my office, comfy chairs, pumpkin-scented candle burning, with a good cup of coffee, and time... time to chat, share, learn, question, clarify, and wonder... time together to learn these skills and explore how they apply specifically to you and your relationships.

That is *how* I wrote this book. With a picture of you, the reader, taped to my computer, picturing the scene above. While you may not be a client or in one of my coaching programs yet, we can share some virtual coffee and conversation. Whether I am coaching clients, speaking or teaching about how to create *better* relationships, rekindle your romance, become a confident parent, grow deeper in your faith, or build a strong marriage while growing a successful business—*no matter what the subject is*—I have never met anyone who didn't want to improve one or more of their relationships and just wasn't sure how to go about it.

That is *why* I wrote this book. So no matter what our past or future involvement is or may be, you will have firsthand knowledge of the foundational skills used in all my coaching, speaking, and writing to successfully help people create better relationships.

Listen, Learn, Love can be universally applied to all of your relationships: loved ones, spouse, partner, significant other, kids (and yes… even teens), parents, siblings, friends, and coworkers. Why? Because they address the core needs of all good relationships. We all long to be seen, heard, known, loved, and feel valued.

In the movie *Shall We Dance* there is a scene in which Beverly Clark, the wife of the main character, John, is talking with a private detective who has been investigating if her husband is being unfaithful. The PI meets Beverly to report that John is not a wayward spouse. His strange absences and behavior are because he is taking dance lessons. Mystified by John's secrecy, Beverly gets misty-eyed and quiet. After a few moments of reflection, she asks the PI if he knows why people get married. He offers a banal reply. Shaking her head, Beverly softly replies, "*We get married because we want someone to bear witness to our lives. We want to know that we matter.*"

In our quiet moments, maybe late at night when we can't fall asleep, or the wee hours of the morning alone with our coffee and the breaking dawn, we know it's true… We are hardwired for connection. We can't escape the fact that we are created for relationship. We want to belong, to know we matter.

What an elegant and wise way to express the reason we willingly slog through tough and challenging relationships. We hope they get better; we make efforts to improve them and, in our utter optimism, we keep risking in order to develop lasting and meaningful ones.

Think about the relationships in your life that bring you satisfaction, joy, and growth. They probably also have some level of struggle or conflict. Do you throw up your hands and walk away, bury it under the carpet, and hope it gets better, or maybe punt and find a new friend? Wouldn't you agree that none of those is the best solution? Relationships—messy and mediocre to glorious and grand—are the most valuable thing in our lives and worth our investment of time and energy. Join me in exploring how *Listen, Learn, Love* can help.

How to Get the Most from This Book

In the coming chapters, I will unpack each skill with anecdotes and examples as if we are having a conversation. Together we will walk through some specific examples and tips, followed by ideas and action steps to practice and apply in your own relationships.

Listen, Learn, Love are the tools needed to handle times of conflict and struggle, create better relationships, and improve your quality of life. Relationships are the currency of today. Connecting with people and the ability to build positive and fulfilling relationships are the most important skills we can develop. At work, at home, at play—relationships matter!

Please take the time to put yourself in the scenes and situations described. I have tried to include examples of *Listen, Learn, Love* in multiple types of relationships. As you read, imagine how you would handle the situations, both before and after learning each skill. Practice them by replaying the scenarios in your mind, taking notes, and then actually trying them out in your different relationships. If you use these skills, you will see results. Your personal and professional relationships will dramatically improve. If you don't practice and use them—if you do nothing—then nothing will change.

Take Notes and Make Notes

I would love for you to be engaged in the process. Interaction is the first step towards integration and the goal is to integrate these principles so they become second nature.

If you are a "paper book" reader, go ahead—Break the rules and write in the margins of the book. I mean it! Thoughts, people, and situations will come to mind as you are reading... Jot them down. I like to pretend I will remember the important points or thoughts that come to mind as I am reading, but I don't. So, writing them down is the best solution. Dog-ear the pages that resonate with you; underline things you want to remember; mark up this book! My favorite books are filled with underlining, squiggles, stars, notes, and dog-eared pages, so I can quickly find the most helpful or enjoyable parts.

If you are an "e-book" reader, pick up a journal and take notes, highlight the text and/or make notes on your e-reader. Sync them to Evernote. Do whatever you need to mark areas of interest you want to remember. Either way, let this be an interactive process and you will begin to create the changes you desire in your relationships. Good books, helpful and useful ones, are like friends, visited often to remember, reminisce, and learn from. I hope this book is like that for you.

So grab a pencil, a cup of coffee, and let's get started at learning how you can dramatically improve your personal and professional relationships.

A Few Thoughts before We Dive In

For clarity and brevity I will use one term throughout the book to apply to many:

- Loved ones: anyone you love or care deeply about.
- Spouse: partner, significant other, a committed romantic relationship (when I use a gender-specific pronoun, feel free to substitute the one that fits your life).
- Businessman, businesswoman, entrepreneur (male or female): used interchangeably.
- Business, career, work, entrepreneurial endeavor: used interchangeably.
- Coworker: colleague, business associate, virtual assistant, anyone you work with in any capacity.
- Customer, client, patient (used interchangeably).
- Family: immediate and extended family, siblings, parents, in-laws.
- Friends: close friends you "do life with," not acquaintances, customers or clients.

Anecdotes and Examples

Some are personal stories from my own life. Others are a composite of stories drawn from over 20 years of working with people. None of the examples or anecdotes are an exact representation of any one person, event, or client. I use fictional names and mix up the details in order to protect the privacy of my clients. (So if you think you see yourself in a story, rest assured, it probably isn't you, but rather an amalgamation of client stories woven together to create an example.) Unless you specifically gave me permission to use your story, you aren't in the book. I hold your stories sacred and in confidence.

Relationship Avatar

You know the picture that comes up on your phone when someone calls you? Or their thumbnail photo on Facebook, Twitter, or other social media? Or the little photo that shows up in your Outlook next to an email from them? Well, that picture is their avatar: a visual image or representation of a person. So, your *relationship avatar* is a visual image, picture, or snapshot that comes to mind when you think of a specific relationship. Whenever I reference your *relationship avatar*, I want you to picture that image and the relationship it represents as you read examples, scenarios, and action steps. You can use different relationship avatars from your multiple types of relationships or the same ones for all the skills... It's up to you. The purpose is to personalize this book to your life and relationships so you can begin to make changes and improve them!

Practicing *Listen, Learn, Love*

Unique action steps and application ideas for each skill to use with relationship avatars while you are immersed in the book and then apply them to your various relationships, live and in person. Be bold and give them a try! Remember, change and growth happen by making an effort and taking one step forward... then doing it over and over again! It might encourage you to know I am on this journey with you. In fact, while writing this book a number of relationships and people came to mind, which required me to be bold or humble, and use *Listen, Learn, Love* skills to improve our relationship... So let's grow together!

ListenLearnLoveCommunity.com is there for you.

Come join our community! It's important to know you're not in this alone. I would love to hear about moments of connection, understanding, increased ease, or how practicing and implementing these skills impacted your relationships. And if you feel you need more time, tools, help, or encouragement, our *Listen, Learn, Love* Community is there to support and encourage you on your journey. Remember, we're all in this together. I can't wait to connect and hear your stories!

Chapter 2

Relationships Are the Currency of Today

"Relationships are all there is. Everything in the
universe only exists because it is in relationship to
everything else. Nothing exists in isolation.
We have to stop pretending we are individuals.
We say we exchange words when we meet.
What we exchange is souls."

—Minot J. Savage

Relationships impact every area of our lives. If we want to succeed in this world, we must be able to create meaningful and lasting relationships. Everyone longs to have rewarding personal relationships: enjoyable friendships, a deep and committed love, sustaining and supportive bonds with our kids and family. We also need successful professional relationships. We desire connection; we even try to work at them, but relationships are not always fulfilling, satisfying or going well. Unfortunately, we often settle for average.

We muddle through: more roommates than romance with our spouse, our kids have more interactions with their

Smartphones than with us and sometimes we are too tired to care. Our friendships feel "surfacey," our extended family communicates only when there is a crisis, and our business relationships are more transactional than creative and synergistic... Does this sound familiar?

Have you settled for average when what you really want is awesome or at least *better* relationships? Are you aware of how mediocre, difficult, tension-filled, lonely relationships significantly impact every area of your life? We are emotional beings. Even though we try to be logical and rational, our emotions and feelings intrude, especially those related to our relationships, and spill over into all aspects of our lives.

Take a moment to think about a time when you were happy, content, or had enjoyed some positive aspects in a relationship. How did the rest of your day go? Were you in a better mood? I imagine your outlook was more positive: car windows down, radio on, traffic on the commute wasn't a big deal, work hassles didn't bug you; your day just went smoothly. Maybe your good mood extended into confidence that helped you land a big client, have patience with your teen, or give you extra energy for your spouse.

Difficult relationships have the opposite effect. Most of us have heard the sad but true joke about the man who had a bad day at work... came home and yelled at his wife, who snapped at the kids, who then kicked the dog. The quality of our relationships impacts all areas of our lives.

We don't often consider how intertwined our personal and professional relationships are and how this reality affects us.

Remember a time when personal relationship stress weighed heavily on you and negatively impacted your mood, attitude, and energy at work? Everything was harder: paper jams, paper cuts, cancellations, molehills became mountains, and you felt thwarted and stymied. Creativity is essential for success in life and work. Many of the entrepreneurs and successful business people I coach lament how relationship stress blocks their creativity and efficiency. When our personal relationships are thriving, we are more productive, profitable, and effective at our work. When our work relationships are flourishing, we are more enjoyable at home. Life is simply better on all fronts!

Many successful business executives and entrepreneurs regret their lack of investment in their personal relationships during their climb to the top. Now they are alone with no one to celebrate their victories or share in their success. At home and at work, rewarding and fulfilling relationships are essential to happiness and success.

"You can't truly be considered successful in your business life if your home life is in shambles."
—Zig Ziglar

For all our investments in career training, health, gym memberships, or financial futures, we often forget to invest in the most important and influential things in our lives: relationships. Then we wonder why we are stalled, stuck, moving slowly, unsatisfied, un-energized, or feeling just plain blah.

Relationships Drive Our Choices

Relationships... good ones, easy ones, complex ones and, yes, even hard and challenging ones... fill our lives. Wouldn't you agree relationships motivate most of our life and work choices? They are our "why." Most of us work in order to provide a certain lifestyle for our families; we want to create a better life for them and have the financial freedom to enjoy experiences, as well as give to others in need.

Think about your day—all the moment-by-moment details. How much of it is related to relationships? Schedules, commutes, emails, business meetings, lunches, sales calls, after-school activities, evening commitments, volunteering, recreational pursuits, even entrepreneurial dreams pursued after hours—are all related to the people in our lives.

Relationships are the stuff of life; they are what drive us, sustain us, comfort us, and yes, challenge us. Life without meaningful relationships would be... well, meaningless... dull and empty. Without relationships, I think we would all drift away without passion, purpose, or hope. Relationships tether us to our lives, and add richness and value; they anchor us in our story. I believe learning to create and nurture significant relationships is essential to meaningful, enjoyable, and productive lives.

While relationships are the most important things in our lives, they are usually the hardest. They bring us joy, delight, and purpose, but also pain, sorrow, confusion, grief, frustration, and loneliness. We want great relationships; we would even settle for good. But the work and effort to create and sustain them seems daunting, so we punt. We pretend we aren't lonely and settle for fair to middling relationships, wondering, "Is this all there is?"

Remember when you met your spouse? While you were falling in love, the relationship was wonderful and communication seemed so easy. He loved everything you said, agreed with you, thought you hung the moon! But these days, not so much! You wonder, "What happened? How did we get here? I didn't sign up for this!" After the honeymoon phase, we wake up to reality... Living 24/7 with this person is hard. They get on our nerves; they don't agree with us all the time; they criticize and try to change us.

Most relationships make a shift:

- The sweet baby and tenderhearted toddler disappear into a truculent teen.
- The great boss, who was excited about our new ideas, starts shooting them down and, instead, promotes sticking to the status quo.
- Our supportive spouse wavers in their excitement and commitment to the time and financial cost of pursuing our entrepreneurial dreams.
- Tension floods our friendships with other moms as school politics or sports team selections impact your kids and their friendships.
- Clients become competitors.
- Sibling rivalry, disagreements, and jealousy replace childhood games and treehouse dreams.

Suddenly, building strong relationships and deep connections just got exponentially harder and more complicated. We are tempted to give up. Alternatively, we may try to convince ourselves it isn't "so bad, maybe it will get better," so we sweep our feelings under the rug and power through. But like many other issues or problems we try to ignore, it just gets bigger and soon we are tripping over the huge mound under the carpet.

If relationships are the stuff of life, why are we rarely, if ever, taught how to create quality ones? Growing up we are taught to be polite, not make waves, apologize, use our words instead of our fists, but we really never learn the necessary skills for building strong and lasting relationships. We don't take classes on how to communicate. Sure, we learn to talk; we even learn big words and how to give public speeches, but we are not taught the essential skill of how to communicate effectively or create thriving relationships. When an unexpected crisis hits, our relationships deteriorate or become difficult at best.

Suddenly, we realize our communication and relationship skills need work. Usually we don't seek help or actively learn how to develop healthy and enjoyable relationships until a problem arises. Reactively, we seek out seminars, coaches, and workshops, but by this time we are already in crisis and behind the eight ball. Doesn't it make more sense to do a little skill development and learning on the front end? Especially if it equips us to avoid the emotional upheaval that often accompanies our forging ahead blindly or with hubris! *Listen, Learn, Love* cannot only help us create better relationships, but also equip us to handle crisis and struggle when they arise. And they will.

> *"You can kiss your family and friends goodbye and put miles between you, but at the same time you carry them with you in your heart, your mind, your stomach, because you do not just live in a world but a world lives in you."*
> —*Frederick Buechner*

Everyone Struggles, Even Professionals

In 2013, our adult daughter (our middle child) went on *The World Race*, an 11-month mission trip, traveling to 11 countries in 11 months. This quotation was never truer for me than during that time. The meaning was heightened because our relationship was strained before she left. It was normal "mother/mid-twenties daughter" stuff, nothing relationship-shattering, but not the way a mom wants to say goodbye to her child as she leaves for almost a year. I wished I understood why we clashed, and what I did that frustrated, disappointed, and just plain bugged her. Maybe then I could figure out a way to just stop doing it! We had talked about our relationship… calmly at times… with tension at others.

I wanted to force the issue before she left. Thankfully, my hubby and my mom suggested I hold it loosely, give her space, and trust God. Was it hard? You bet! I cried… a lot. I tried to be lighthearted as we packed and spent time together during those last few days. I am sure my longing for it to be different leaked out and she felt pressure. She was gracious. I tried to be patient and quiet, sharing the bulk of my thoughts, fears, worries, and questions with God, my hubby, and mom. They reminded me to have faith. I struggled.

As we hugged one last time, my heart ached. I knew I had blown it—I tried to have conversations, got frustrated, hurt her feelings, shared too much, said too little, and now she was leaving... for 11 months. Sure there would be FaceTime, texts, and emails, but they would be short, newsy, and light. It would be a year before we could really talk about anything. Our relationship struggles weighed heavy on my heart as she trekked the world. Of course, I hoped and prayed she would return home safely, but also that we could share openly, mend fences, deal with the tension, address my alienating actions or words, and build a stronger relationship.

She is home again and when I take my own advice and *Listen, Learn* her, and *Love Well*, I can see things improving between us. (Amazing how that works!) I am learning to *listen* in the ways I teach, but can fail miserably at living out. I am *learning* her bit by bit... how she is different from what I may think or assume based on her childhood years. Her adult experiences have impacted and shaped her as well. I am trying to *Love Well* by being patient and quiet, and giving her space, which is sometimes very hard for me. I want to just hash it out, figure out how to fix it; I wanted to do it my way... but then, the skill of *loving well* isn't about me.

Using these skills, our relationship has improved. We share some delightful times, great conversations, and times of connection reminiscent of her younger years. We are learning to accept and enjoy each other. It's ironic; we both want a deep and connected relationship... We are just figuring out how to have one as adults. I am hopeful and grateful. She is patient and forgiving. (So to all the moms reading... don't lose heart; life is long and relationships with our kids survive the teens and twenties!)

Does knowing I struggle in my relationships give you hope and encouragement? It should! Seriously, I teach this stuff— This is my wheelhouse and I struggle, falter, and fail! Not all my relationships are thriving, awesome, and without conflict. Creating better relationships is a process. There is hope!

Sometimes when I am coaching clients, I hear myself encourage them to specifically use one of these skills to handle an issue or improve their relationship. And I hear a voice in the back of my head chuckle and say, "So are you the pot or the kettle today?"

In addition to my own experiences, I have learned a great deal from the privilege of helping my clients build *better* relationships with themselves, God, and others. As we dive into their stories, relational struggles, and questions, we work together to improve their connections as they practice skills and change unproductive habits or patterns of relating. They begin to see substantial improvements where they have often given up hope.

On a shelf in my office, I have a pair of child-sized, bright yellow rain boots. They are a gift from a couple to symbolize my "walking through the mud with them and helping them grow a strong, intimate, and enjoyable marriage." Every time I see the boots, I smile and am grateful this is what I get to do with my life! Through my journeys with others, I have seen numerous clients create remarkable progress in their relationships with loved ones and friends! With this in mind, I encourage you to engage with this book. Ponder the quotations, put yourself into the examples, "try on" the three skills and do the practice exercises and begin to use *Listen, Learn, Love* in your relationships.

An easy way to "try on" these skills is to create a relationship avatar (a visual image, picture, or snapshot that comes to mind to represent your specific relationship). Remember, you can use the same relationship avatar with all the skills or choose different ones—to represent different relationships in your life—throughout the book. It's up to you. The purpose is to put a face and a real relationship into the context of each skill and then envision implementing them and imagine how doing so will impact your relationship.

You can make changes and dramatically improve your relationships if you are willing to learn and practice these skills. Just begin… and then continue… one step at a time.

Practicing *Listen, Learn, Love*

1. Think for a moment about your relationships and bring to mind the faces of friends or loved ones who fit into one or more of these categories:

- Your relationship is marked by tension, disagreement or struggle.
- You are settling for a mediocre relationship.
- You want to develop a deeper connection.
- You just want to have a better relationship (define what "better" means to you).

These people are your relationship avatars.

2. Consider the value of these relationships and commit to the process of taking one or more of them through the various action steps in this book. You can use a single relationship or choose a different relationship to focus on for each skill.

3. As you read, I encourage you to be open-minded and optimistic, to invest the time to process the information with specific relationships in mind.

   - Envision yourself in the different scenarios throughout the book.
   - Interact with this book, take notes, and do the action steps. It will be a bit like collaborating with me in a coaching session. As you learn and use these skills, you will enjoy dynamic connections and improved relationships.

Please share how practicing and implementing these skills impacted your relationships on our Listen, Learn, Love Community page at www.ListenLearnLoveCommunity.com/stories.

Chapter 3

Hearing Without *Listening*

"The most basic of all human needs is the need to understand and be understood. The best way to understand people is to listen to them."
—Ralph Nichols

Skill #1: Listen

When I chose the name of this skill, I could imagine one of my mentors saying, "Well, duh?!" with crinkly, twinkling eyes and a wise smile on her lined face. She had a way of cutting to the chase. When you read *Skill #1: Listen*, did you think the same thing? I can imagine your inner dialogue: "Everyone knows that listening is important to relationships. How can this be one of the 'super-secret,' foolproof, elegant, and effective skills that will literally change my relationships? I listen all the time!"

Do you?

Honestly, most of us don't really listen very well. Oh,

we hear words, but listening is far more than hearing the words as they enter our brains, while we are figuring what to say in response. *Listening* requires focus, attentiveness, and pausing long enough to really engage in what someone else is communicating.

> *"The most important thing in communication*
> *is to hear what isn't being said."*
> —Peter F. Drucker

Will Smith plays the main character, Alex Hitchens, in a great movie about relationships titled *Hitch.* He tutors single men in connecting and creating a genuine relationship with the woman of their dreams. The movie opens with a montage of men struggling and failing miserably in their pursuit of a relationship.

During the opening scene, Hitch, as he is called, does a voice-over tutorial on communication saying, "Her words are, 'Now isn't a good time for me... I need space... I'm really into my career right now.' She's lying to you. She doesn't want to hurt your feelings. Sixty percent of communication is nonverbal body language; thirty percent is tone, and how you say it. That means that ninety percent of what you're saying isn't coming out of your mouth."

The scene offers a powerful visual about the reality of nonverbal communication. I show this scene at all of my marriage seminars or retreats, and it's a crowd-pleaser as everyone relates to how messed up communicating can get!

(Rent the movie; you won't regret it!) We hear words all the time, but do we really *listen* with our ears and eyes to the entire message delivery in order to comprehend the meaning? Body language and facial expressions, as well as tone, combine with words to influence our message. No wonder communication is challenging!

Picture a time with a friend sharing something exciting in your life: upcoming travel plans, a promotion at work, an awesome business idea, a new romance—and you could tell from their facial expression and posture they were just waiting for you to finish so they could shoot it down, poke holes in it, or chime in with the proverbial, "Me too!"

Conversation over! You sat back and let them ramble on, and thought, "They aren't even listening. Are they really interested in me and my life? Do they care about what I have to say, or do they just want to talk about themselves?"

Ouch... the sting, loneliness, and disappointment in that moment—sucks! However, if you're anything like me—or the general public, for that matter—and willing to be honest, you can picture yourself on both sides of that conversation. Frequently, we "hear," but we don't really *listen*, take in, and process what the other person is communicating in their words, tone, and body language.

Quite often, while we are hearing the words, what is registering in our minds is "whaa-whaa-whaa," a bit like Charlie Brown's teacher, while we are busy crafting our response. We are so busy with our own thoughts, we don't pay attention or really listen to the message being communicated. Listening means we put aside what we think they are saying and pay attention to what they are actually saying. A great way to listen and communicate our desire to understand is to treat the person speaking as if they are the most important person in the room.

> *"When people talk, listen completely.*
> *Most people never listen."*
> *—Ernest Hemingway*

Listening is not:
- A defense, dismissal, or explanation: "Well, this is why I did/said/acted that way."
- Rebuttal or unloading: "Well you, did/said/acted in a way that hurt me."
- "Me too" stories: "Really? Me too, in fact when I… blah, blah, blah… me, me, me!"

This is a skill I am still practicing and trying to master, especially "me too" stories. Sometimes, I get so excited and in my desire to connect with people, I jump in and hijack the conversation. Recently, on a couples date night, a friend was sharing about his trip to Paris; I kept joining in with my thoughts and experiences. Me, me, and more me… is not being a good listener! The better option: be quiet, simply nod in agreement, and enter the discussion with questions about my friend's experience. (I teach this skill and still forget to use it sometimes, so don't beat yourself up if you need more practice, too!)

Listening is:
- Pausing and taking time to let what the other person is saying sink in.
- Asking questions for more information and clarity.
- Paying attention to their nonverbal communication.

Molly and Bill came for a couples coaching intensive. While discussing a difficult issue, they reached an impasse—unable to hear or validate the hurt in each other's tone and words because they were afraid acknowledging the other's hurt meant taking responsibility and claiming intentionality in causing pain. As we worked to understand the concept of listening and taking in what their spouse was saying, I could literally see their bodies relax.

I smiled as Bill turned to Molly and said, "Hmm, I can see how my staying longer at work, especially after saying I was just leaving, led to your feeling unappreciated and disrespected; that was not my intention."

Molly's face softened; with a big sigh she replied, "I know you didn't do it on purpose." Their conversation began to flow as defenses came down and both partners listened to each other.

Listening reduces tension in a heated moment by demonstrating our desire to understand. We desperately want to feel heard, and to know our thoughts, feelings, or experiences matter to others.

Tips to Practice Skill #1: Listen

Learning, practicing, and mastering *Skill #1: Listen* will make a huge difference in creating relational ease and enjoyment. Let's discuss a few tips to better equip you to use this skill effectively.

Pause & Pay Attention

Tip #1: Pause; stop thinking about what you want to say in response and pay attention to nonverbal cues.

Pausing allows time for their message to sink in. It improves your ability to listen and understand what is being communicated. Pausing is extremely helpful when the conversation is tense or conflictual. When we feel listened to and understood, often the intensity drops, the tension shifts, and resolution is easier to attain.

Pausing is sometimes challenging for me. My mind runs at warp speed and I use words for a living! I have to consciously slow my brain down and *listen...* to the words and the message behind them, as well as what is *not* being said, plus pay attention to the nonverbal cues. As a counselor and coach, I have trained myself to pause, ponder, and intentionally focus my mind on *all* that is being communicated, not what I will say in response. (I don't always do as this well with my family and friends, but I continue to practice!)

Stop thinking about what you want to say in response, especially when the conversation is difficult. When a friend or loved one comes to you with an issue that is bothering them, do everything in your power to pause and *listen.* Usually we offer a quick defense, explanation, and/or a "well you did such and such" comeback. When we feel defensive or are itching to explain ourselves, we often check out of the conversation and begin to craft our retort. Our inner defense lawyer rears her head, and in minutes we have our opening argument ready to go. Resist this natural tendency! Remember, they had the courage to come to you and share something difficult. Honor this by really listening and staying focused on their message. This is not the time to bring up a problem or struggle you may have with them. Have the guts to address your issue on a different day, after their concerns are addressed.

Using this tip can reduce the number and volume of your arguments. (Or "discussions," as we called them when our kids were younger and overheard us. But I don't think we fooled them a bit!)

Pay attention to both verbal and nonverbal communication to gain a deeper understanding of their message. Far more is being communicated with tone, body language, and expressions.

Has your wife ever replied, "I'm fine!" in a frustrated, one-octave-higher tone of voice when you asked her, "How are you doing?" But… everything about her screamed, "Oh no, I'm not!" Her arms crossed as she glared at you with knitted brow and pursed lips... (not for kissing either!) Because you were paying attention, you realized she was really communicating: "You should read my mind and know that I am not fine, even though I said I am!" (Humorous, but it happens often.)

Paying attention to *all* the incoming data will help you discern the full message being communicated.

> *"You cannot truly listen to anyone and*
> *do anything else at the same time."*
> *—M. Scott Peck*

Fire Your Defense Attorney

Tip #2: Clarify & Validate.

Learn to ask "Hmmm… Can you tell me more about that?" or be willing to say, "Help me understand what you mean?" or "What was that like for you?" in response to someone sharing their thoughts and feelings. For example, imagine your wife is frustrated and feels disrespected because you contradicted or changed some consequences she gave your kids. At this moment, your job is to become a crack investigator; ask questions to clarify exactly what she means and feels.

Then, instead of justifying, explaining, or defending yourself—affirm or validate her feelings. She wants to be heard, understood, and supported.

Clarifying and validating says, "You matter enough for me to make the effort to understand what you are trying to communicate." Validating her feelings does not mean you agree with them; it means you understand what she is feeling and why she feels this way. This is an important distinction when both people are convinced their thoughts, feelings, or actions are right. The point is not *who* is right, but you (the reader of the book) being willing to validate what they (the person you want a better relationship with) are feeling. Clarifying and validating enables you to engage in their message, not in your rebuttal or reasoning.

This is one of my favorite things to teach couples and families when we first start working together because practicing this skill brings rapid results. Asking a loved one to expand on how we have hurt, frustrated, or disappointed them is not usually our knee-jerk reaction. And validating their feelings is not the first thing on our minds when someone shares why they are less than pleased with us.

Try it sometime. Look at your frustrated spouse, disappointed kid, irate coworker and instead of defending or explaining, say, "Hmmm, tell me more about that; help me understand what I did or didn't do that made you feel this way." They will probably be surprised you weren't defensive. They may go off on a tirade. Hang in there. Your job is to listen. This one tweak in your response can change the conversation and begin to improve your relationship quickly.

Clarifying and validating someone else's feelings requires lowering our defenses and listening, even if it is hard. Doing so communicates your desire to deal with their concern and repair the relationship. After data-gathering, reflective listening is a great technique to clarify and confirm that you are correct in what you *think* they are saying.

Reflective listening means you reply with your understanding of their message. You might say, "What I hear you saying is…" This ensures you accurately understand their message. They can clarify or expand. Continue doing this until their response is, "Yes, that is what I am saying!" We feel safe when someone makes an effort to understand our thoughts and feelings, when our relationship is strong enough to handle real emotions and issues. Think about a time when someone validated your feelings instead of trying to talk you out of them, diminish them, or even dismiss them. A time when you really felt listened to and understood. I imagine you thought, "Wow, this is awesome!" When you listen, you offer this same feeling to your spouse, kids, friends, family, and colleagues, and doing so helps create better relationships.

> *"The greatest compliment that was ever paid me was when one asked me what I thought, and attended to my answer."*
> —Henry David Thoreau

What About My Feelings?

Feelings are. Period. End of sentence. We cannot control our feelings. We can only control what we do with our feelings. In my work with clients we talk a lot about "feeling your feelings" and *then* deciding what you want to do about them. Too often we mishandle our feelings. Judged as inappropriate, we try to deny, change, or bury them; this simply does not work. It is a bit like trying to hold a beach ball under water... it always pops up somewhere. Feelings are similar. We try to hide, deny or stuff them. Then we overreact about a small issue: we snap at our kids, find fault with a coworker... or we are just plain cranky. Ignored feelings, like beach balls, will pop up somewhere. Usually at inopportune moments, creating an even bigger mess! We need to express our feelings and allow others to do the same.

When someone shares their feelings, the best thing to do is validate them—whether or not we agree with them—instead of trying to talk someone out of their feelings or "help" change them.

One day our outgoing son came home from middle school and said, "I don't have any friends." Perplexed by this statement because he was a pretty popular kid, I did the absolutely wrong thing and replied, "Yes, you do," and proceeded to list a few. Talk about a conversation-killer! He didn't feel listened to, heard or understood. I dismissed his feelings. He felt shut down, said, "Whatever!" and walked away.

I blew it.

I was so caught up in not wanting him to feel this way (my feelings), that I missed an opportunity to validate his feelings and discover the story behind them. I hope the next time he struggled, I responded with, "Sorry you feel that way... That sucks," and then proceeded to ask questions and listen to what he was trying to communicate. But as a work in progress, I messed up often with all my kids. Please don't judge yourself on your missteps or failures. Instead, give yourself credit for learning and practicing these skills. Change takes time. I applaud your courage to enter the arena of growth and your willingness to try. Like any skill, the more you practice, the better you become. So keep practicing.

Allowing a loved one to express their feelings, then seeking to clarify and validate them, is a terrific way to show you care and will strengthen your relationship.

The Most Important Question to Ask

Tip #3: Learn to Say "I'm Sorry."

Be willing to be wrong. "I'm sorry" are two of the most powerful and effective words in the English language!

My friend's daughter, Stephanie, and her fiànce, Dustin, were deep in the midst of plans for their upcoming wedding.

It was a Saturday, and they were running errands and making final decisions about the major details of the ceremony and reception. Needless to say, they were tired and stressed.

They were in Dustin's truck and Steph looked over at him and said, "I know there are lots of details to get worked out but one thing is really important to me. I'd like to get a nice wedding band."

Dustin looked over and said, "Why? That seems stupid."

She heard the contempt in his voice. But she quietly said, "There are a lot of things that I don't care about but I think having a nice wedding band is important."

He looked over at her and said, "Don't you think you're being a little ridiculous?"

"Well, I've always wanted a nice wedding band," she said.

Dustin said, "I just don't get it. I think it's stupid."

At this point tears started filling up in her eyes. She said,

"I'm just trying to tell you this is really important to me." She got really quiet and turned her head towards the window.

Dustin could sense she was upset and said, "Look. I'm just saying I think you're being ridiculous."

Steph said, "If it's a matter of money, I can contribute."

"That's even more stupid," he said as his fists tightened on the wheel.

Now tears were rolling down her cheeks and they were both quiet.

She finally broke the silence and said, "It's something I'm going to have my whole life and I just thought it would be good to get a nice one."

"Your whole life? It's just one night and I think it's a waste to spend money on a wedding band that's just for one night."

"Wait? One night? I'm talking about a wedding band... to go with my engagement ring, not a wedding band to play at the reception!"

"Really?" he said. "I'm sorry."

Dusin paused and looked tenderly at Steph. "This whole time, I thought you were talking about a wedding band to play music at the reception."

"No, silly! I was talking about a ring!" she said as a smile beamed on her face, and they both burst out laughing.

Two words—*I'm sorry*—can change everything. In a moment the tension fades, perspectives shift, communication and connection deepen; the relationship is restored.

I'm sorry is *not* saying, "You are absolutely right; I am a jerk and I did that on purpose." It is saying, "I'm sorry you are hurting and that my action/words or lack of action contributed to those feelings; it was not my intention to hurt you."

A crucial question is: *Is being right more important than this relationship?* I encourage you to ask yourself this question often in the midst of a tense conversation or disagreement. Remembering this question reminds me the relationship is most important and helps me practice *Listen, Learn, Love*, especially when I don't want to. It has kept me from making a difficult situation worse and reminded me to be willing to say I'm sorry. Knowing this truth and putting it into practice often seems like crossing the Grand Canyon. We falsely view being the first to apologize as a sign of weakness or as caving in. What if you reframed the choice to be the first to say, I'm sorry as a sign of strength and humility? You willingly relinquish the demand to be right, communicating that this person and your relationship is more important. Can you imagine how your relationships would improve?

"I'm sorry" is not an admission of guilt. It is *not* declaring you purposely did or said something wrong or are taking responsibility for what you may be accused of doing. Sometimes it simply acknowledges their hurt and your sorrow for their struggle. It *is* giving them a place to share their feelings and your impact on them.

Denial Makes It Worse

I am a cancer survivor and the treatment to kill the cancer resulted in a compromised immune system and 10 subsequent years of chronic illness. I have great doctors, take all kinds of vitamins, and work hard to stay well. But sometimes to fight debilitating infections, I must take high doses of steroids, which give me insomnia and alter my personality. One year it got so bad, I hardly recognized myself—bloated from steroid-induced weight gain, frazzled from stress and insomnia, battling sadness, depression, and steroid mania—I was a wreck. Living in denial (yes, coaches and therapists have issues too), I would make plans, pretending that maybe tomorrow I would feel better... only to cancel them in the morning.

Desperately wanting my life to be different, I continued in this cycle. However, I didn't take into account how living in denial impacted the people in my life. I will never forget a difficult interaction with our oldest daughter. She was angry and disappointed because I was feeling physically awful, and had cancelled our plans... again.

She shared her frustration and I snapped back at her. She was legitimately disappointed. I had foolishly made plans when it was likely I wouldn't be able to follow through. Both of us were angry about the impact of my illness on our lives. Due to the steroids, my temper and patience were short and insomnia had frazzled my very last nerve. She looked at me and said, "It's really hard to be mad at you for cancelling plans because you are sick... or for the way you act and hurt my feelings when I know it's because you are so sick and on medicine that changes you."

Bam...

She was mature, courageous, and honest about her struggles and feelings. What is a good response to her tender vulnerability? She was hurting and angry. Her feelings were valid. She wanted me to understand and stop changing plans. She wanted me to be well.

This was one of my better mom moments and rather than explaining, dismissing or justifying, I said, "I'm sorry. That must be really hard for you and it totally sucks that you have to deal with this."

Big sigh... Her posture changed as if a weight had been lifted off. She felt heard, listened to, and validated... just what she needed. It didn't fix the problem or even change the situation, but an ease came over our relationship as she realized I understood, accepted, validated, and even apologized for my part in her frustration and struggle.

I hated being sick. I despised the medicines and their impact on my body, mind, personality, and life. I was angry at cancer, at life, at myself, and at God. I felt out of control and in many areas I was. I couldn't get better faster or change the way the steroids or illness affected me, but living in denial was hurting the people I loved. I realized what gave me hope just set my daughter and others up for disappointment. I tried to stop making plans based more on my desire than reality. My daughter was forgiving.

Honestly, I often fail in these kinds of interactions. Explaining and justifying are my right and left hooks when I am feeling defensive; they are devastating blows to communication. But that time, I listened, and it really helped us be gentler with one another in the midst of an extremely difficult season. The words "I'm sorry" go a long way in creating strong and safe relationships. Use these words often. Be willing to say them first. Ask yourself the crucial question: *Is being right more important than this relationship?* Doing this will dramatically improve your relationships in 30 days or less. Try it!

Listen with Your Eyes and Ears

Listening with your eyes, ears, and heart is a foolproof way to develop deep and meaningful relationships. Why? Because most people don't feel listened to and everyone wants to be seen, heard, and understood—not necessarily agreed with, but acknowledged and listened to!

Have you ever been wounded by the words or actions of a close friend? Imagine yourself driving to Starbucks to meet for a cup of coffee. It's hard to envision not being defensive and guarded. Sitting there drinking lattes, you wonder, "Should I mention anything? Maybe I'm overreacting or being too sensitive." (Of course, she's busy sharing, while all this runs through your mind.) Suddenly she pauses, puts down her coffee cup, reaches over, touches your arm, looks you directly in the eyes and asks, "Is something bothering you? You seem distracted, distant…" Wouldn't that be awesome? She is listening to *all* you are communicating and inviting you to share what's bothering you. She's a close and trusted friend, so you share your thoughts and feelings. She had no idea her words had injured her dear friend and is glad you told her… apologies, misty eyes, laughter, and restoration. You are relieved and grateful as your relationship grows deeper, safer, and stronger.

> *"I feel it shelter to speak to you."*
> —Emily Dickinson

Imagine if...

- Picture a conversation with your aging parents; they don't want to face the fact they are aging, let alone have a conversation about it. However, they realize you're worried about future plans or what their preferences would be should they become disabled. They not only validate your worry, but also willingly have a conversation they prefer to avoid.

- Envision a discussion with your spouse about a necessary debt increase for your entrepreneurial dream. Instead of fearfully shaking their head or just blurting out, "No!" your spouse said, "Okay, even though it scares me, help me understand the need for this investment because I want to be supportive."

- What if during a work meeting a colleague noticed your body language communicated frustration but you hadn't spoken up, and he paused to ask for your thoughts and input?

Jot down some thoughts and feelings that came to mind as you read each of these scenarios. How do you feel when someone really listens to you?

To create better relationships, we must be the ones who practice *Skill #1: Listen*. Like the conch shell we pick up to hear the ocean and return to the shore in our mind's eye, listening opens us to a deeper understanding of others. We will discover a multitude of insights, points of connection, and stories about our loved ones, friends, and colleagues that will help you create better relationships.

Practicing *Listen, Learn, Love*

1. Pick one of your relationship avatars and recall a recent conversation when you did a less-than-stellar job of listening. Maybe you jumped in with "Me too," and hijacked the conversation, interrupted to correct an inconsistency or error as they recounted a shared event, or didn't pause and pay attention. Regardless of details, you didn't really listen. If you had a do-over, what would the conversation look and sound like using *Skill #1: Listen*? Write a few notes about how you hope the conversation would go this time!

   If you are really feeling bold, mention it the next time you are with this friend. You might say, "I was thinking about our conversation and I didn't really listen well. I'm sorry. I am working on being a better listener." As their jaw drops open, just smile and know you have begun to build a better relationship with them.

2. Call to mind one conversation where saying "I'm sorry" could have changed the outcome. Write down this person's name—quick, before you talk yourself out of it! Revisit that conversation, call them, show up at their home, office, or school, or take them to coffee, and be brave enough to say, "I'm sorry my actions/words hurt you."

   Remember to ask yourself: *Is being right more important than this relationship?*

3. This week, be aware of how you do or don't listen. Pick one tip and practice it in one or more of your relationships. Over time add a second tip and so on, until you are implementing all the tips and beginning to master *Skill #1: Listen.*

4. Write one specific tip on three Post-it™ notes: Put one on your bathroom mirror, steering wheel, TV remote, or other places you see multiple times each day. They will remind you to take action. I used to think this was silly, but life is full of distractions and often, out of sight is out of mind! When I tried this sticky-note trick, it worked!! Seeing them prompted me to act rather than just think, talk, or dream about it. I ask my clients to use this tool and when they do their relationships improve!

5. Continue to practice *Skill #1: Listen* and watch your relationships improve!

Please share how practicing and implementing these skills impacted your relationships on our Listen, Learn, Love Community page at www.ListenLearnLoveCommunity.com/stories.

Chapter 4
Treasure Hunts

"Truth is, I'll never know all there is to know about you, just as you will never know all there is to know about me. Humans are by nature too complicated to be understood fully. So we can choose either to approach our fellow human beings with suspicion or to approach them with an open mind, a dash of optimism, and a great deal of candor."
—Tom Hanks

Skill #2: Learn Them

One of my closest friends is Southern, and one day while talking about her new husband she said, "I just have to learn him." I wasn't sure exactly what she meant; it was a new term for this Northern gal. She explained, "This simply means learning about him: understanding his ways, preferences, styles of giving and showing love, his moods, when he is angry, hungry, discouraged, tired, excited... *Learn him* means really know him!"

I love this term.

Learn Them perfectly captures the process of discovery

essential to any thriving relationship. *Learning people* creates deeper connections. Isn't it restful and gratifying when someone really knows you, gets you, and enjoys you? We find comfort in familiarity. Isn't it heartwarming when your friend brings you a cup of coffee just the way you like it? You realize she paid attention to your likes, dislikes, preferences. Feeling known has a positive impact on the way you interact and strengthens your relationship.

We are created for authentic relationships, deep and meaningful connections, where we let down our guard, remove our masks, turn off the filter, relax, and show our real selves. Have you ever done that? Have you ever spent time with someone and been totally *you*? Uncensored: you didn't have to be "on," or carefully weigh each word or monitor your mood… where instead of a chess game, your time together resembled a ramble down the lazy river: comfortable, easy, and safe? Authentic relationships are restful.

Skill #2: Learn Them will dramatically improve any relationship. It communicates: "You matter. You are worth investing my time and effort to know you more fully." What's more… it's fun! *Learning* your loved ones is a lifelong expedition. There is always something new to discover and enjoy.

"A person isn't who they are during the last conversation you had with them—they're who they've been throughout your whole relationship."
—Rainer Maria Rilke

We often fool ourselves into thinking we really know the important people in our lives, when what we actually have is an image of who we *think* they are—which can have gaps or even be inaccurate. Peering into a kaleidoscope, we see an image. If we averted our eyes and didn't investigate further, we would miss the richness and, quite frankly, the purpose of the kaleidoscope. However, if we continue to look and adjust the lens, we would see this slightest turn creates ever-changing patterns, colors with shifting images, and nuanced beauty, a whole new dimension altogether. The process of discovering and *learning* people on a deep and personal level is similar. God made each of us unique, complex, and multifaceted. As life unfolds, we grow, change, evolve, and become. *Learning* someone is never boring. People are complex and fascinating!

Think about how deeply you really know the important people in your life. What comes to mind? Their shoe size, favorite candy, movie, coffee preference, favorite meal, book, vacation spot? Fun things, yes—but have you *learned them*: their hopes, fears, tendencies, strengths, weaknesses, joys, and struggles? *Learning Them* involves intentionally seeking out below-the-surface revelations. What are their dreams, struggles, experiences—in essence, what is their story, what makes them tick, and how are they unique?

> *"The real voyage of discovery consists not in seeking new landscapes, but in having new eyes."*
> —Marcel Proust

Learn Them **is not:**

- Figuring out the things you would like to change about your spouse, friends, loved ones, or coworkers and developing a plan or campaign to do so.
- Tweaking, correcting, or making negative comments regarding what you learned.
- Invading their privacy, demanding answers and revelations rather than paying attention to clues.

My hubby enjoys watching sports… all sports. *Learning him* means knowing that after a stressful week, watching sports and napping is often his idea of a perfect Sunday afternoon. *Learning him* means not only accepting this about him, but also respecting it and not making comments about how I might think it is a waste of time or planning something else for us to do instead. *Learning him* means I make my own plans on Sunday afternoons or discuss potential couple plans in advance. Sometimes, *learning him* means hanging out on the couch watching the game with him. *Learning me* means he DVRs some games and joins me on some Sunday outings. However, all bets are off during the World Cup!

(This sounds so amicable and lovely; however, it was not always this way. We have worked hard on *Learn Them* and doing so has greatly improved our marriage!)

Learn Them **is:**

- Studying them, observing nonverbal clues, going on a treasure hunt.

- Asking questions, listening to their answers, and seeking out stories.
- Watching and investigating... Go all CSI on them and see what you can dig up.

Very few of us feel deeply known. Marriages in the United States are filled with lonely people, living like roommates and co-existing on a surface level with the "love of their life." We are created for deep connection on a soul or spiritual level, and this happens when we *learn them*... when we take time to put aside our agenda, our multitasking, and fully pay attention. We check our eyes, adjust our vision, get out our "perspectacles," and look for hidden treasures.

Sadly, most of us don't feel known or have a deep sense of belonging. Can you relate? How did you picture your life when you were younger? Are you enjoying the life and relationships you dreamed about and anticipated when you couldn't wait to grow up? For most of us, the honest answer is "No, not really." Or we may be able to say, "Well, some... kinda." But my guess is we would all raise our hands if asked, "Who wants a better relationship with their spouse, kid, family, friends, clients, or coworkers?"

Good news: When we take the time to see with new eyes, to investigate and discover more about our loved ones, understanding increases and connections deepen. Relationships get better! (Maybe not fairy-tale quality, but meaningful and rewarding we can do!)

Reality Check: If your relationships are going to grow and change, you must be the one to take action. Once you begin to use *Skill #2: Learn Them* with just one or two of the most important people in your life, you will see a positive shift in those relationships.

For example:

- You may notice your spouse is weary and a bit short-tempered on Tuesdays: their busiest day of sales calls and potential rejections. After dinner, you take charge, delegate dish duty, get the kids ready for bed, and give them instructions to simply relax and unwind.

- Or, maybe your sister is distant and distracted on the phone. Instead of making small talk, you boldly break the family "don't ask, don't tell" rule and blurt out, "Okay, what's going on? I can tell something is bothering you." However, she avoids your question. Your sister doesn't like discussing uncomfortable things and is very private. Plus, she isn't going to break the family rule. You know this because you *learned her*, so instead of forcing the conversation, you drop it. But the next day, you pop a card in the mail telling her she is in your thoughts and to call if she needs or wants to talk.

In both scenarios, you practiced *Learn Them* to express your care and concern, which always improves relationships.

What about friendships? We comment and post on Facebook and Instagram, tweet, and blog, but we still feel disconnected and lonely. We go out with friends, attend cocktail parties, ladies' lunches or networking events and do the chitchat surface conversations. You know the shtick. We rarely get beyond the *How are you? Great. How are you? Doing good!*

Dead silence. Take a sip of your beer. Scan the room for a diversion.

Instead of a boring two-minute exchange of pleasantries, what if you had a few *Learn Them* questions tucked away to communicate your interest and take your interaction to the next level?

What if *"How was your weekend?" "Great"* progressed to *"Really? Why, what was great about your weekend?"* followed by *"How did you get into doing that?"* As they share, you begin to *learn them*, improving your connection and taking the relationship to a deeper level.

How would life improve if we took the time to genuinely get to know the people in our life… to *learn them* and then engage based on what we learn?

A former client, Ella, married into a family who loved adventure and trying new experiences. She would often email them ideas, event calendars, or Groupons, even though it wasn't really "her thing." Ella knew her husband enjoyed adventures with his extended family and she could bless him by being involved in planning them. Her tips and suggestions resulted in some fun trips and relationship-building experiences for them. And he was grateful that she cared for him in this way.

Tips to Practice Skill #2: Learn Them

Skill #2: Learn Them doesn't have to be complicated. However, it does require being intentional and taking time to investigate and remember what you learn. These few tips will equip you to *learn* the people in your life.

Love Banks

Tip #1: Learn their love languages

The 5 Love Languages™ is an excellent book by Gary Chapman, and the foundation for this tip. The book teaches five different ways we give and receive love. I use this concept with all of my clients and have seen incredible and rapid results. Relationships grow and thrive when we learn how to express our love and care for others in their specific love language, as well as teach others our love language. According to Chapman, *the five love languages* are gifts, words of affirmation, acts of service, quality time, and physical touch.

I highly recommend this book. Simply put: Buy it. Read it. Use it! In the meantime, here are the ways I teach these love languages to my clients:

- *Gifts*: small tokens of affection, cards, flowers, notes, anything that says, "*I was thinking about you—and made this, picked this, or bought this for you.*"
- *Words of affirmation*: words spoken or written —often—that affirm, praise, and offer encouragement.
- *Acts of service*: caring, helpful, or kind acts done on behalf of another.

- *Quality time*: chunks of uninterrupted time, while being fully present and engaged—no smartphones or multitasking.
- *Physical touch* (this is not the same as liking sex): loves to hold hands, sit close, is touchy-feely.

Do you see yourself in any of these? Pause and think about a time you expressed love, care, or appreciation to your spouse, family, or friends. What action did you take? Did you buy flowers or a treat, pick up their dry cleaning or do another kindness, give them a back rub, spend a chunk of time focused on them or doing an activity of their choice, or share your appreciation in words? Once you have an answer, go back and see what category it fits into. My guess is you just identified your love language. (Make a note of your top two love languages.)

We tend to show our love for others in *our* specific love language. This makes us feel great! But we miss the fact that people in our relationships probably have a different love language. *Learning Them* means discovering and using the specific way a loved one, friend, or colleague gives and receives love. Think of using a person's love language as putting money in the bank or making a deposit in their "relationship account." When this account is full rather than empty, there is a lot more grace and understanding when you have to make unexpected withdrawals… also known as disappointments, hurts, misunderstandings, tension, and tough times in a relationship.

The tricky part is we are far more skilled in showing love, care, or appreciation in our preferred language. We often assume our love language is universal. We tend to operate on the misconception that what makes us feel loved, known, and cared for will do the same for others. However, it is more effective to learn and use a person's unique love language to express our care or appreciation. Doing so positively impacts the relationship.

> *"We cannot rely on our native tongue if our spouse does not understand it. If we want them to feel the love we are trying to communicate, we must express it in his or her primary love language."*
> —*Gary Chapman*

I am a "words" girl—encouragement, affirmation, appreciation, and praise make me feel loved and fill my love bank! So my family is rich in love shown through words. I tell my hubby, John: *"I love you," "You're terrific," "You're handsome!"* and foolishly think it fills his love bank. But, John's love language is acts of service. He shows love through kindnesses and care-taking acts. I rarely worry about the nitty-gritty tasks: car inspections, smoke-detector batteries, or keeping the printers stocked with ink. Additionally, he will stop at the grocery store and pick up the things we may be running low on… without my asking! John takes care of me and our family. He is also the financial wizard in the family and CFO of my business.

However, John is not a man of words. It's a running joke in

our home when I will say, *"I love you; you are so amazing!"* And he replies, *"Thanks, but can you put the receipts from your last business trip on my desk so I can finish your financial accounts?"*

Acts of service, not words, would communicate my love to John. Through the years, I learned to do meaningful little things for him, as well as put the receipts on his desk before he asks, and John remembers to say words of encouragement, praise, and affirmation to me!

Early in our marriage, this was not the case. Consequently, our love tanks were often running low, and so were our patience and grace for each other. We both felt misunderstood and unloved. We didn't realize we were speaking two different love languages, and neither of us knew the other's dialect! I spoke mine; he spoke his—lots of misunderstanding! (*Read:* fights, tears, silence, struggle, and fears it wouldn't get better.) After we learned each other's languages and began to use them, our marriage improved!

Learn Them means discovering their love language, then being creative and intentional in expressing your care and love using their language, *not* yours. A shortcut to discovering another person's love language is to watch and observe the way they express love, care, or appreciation to you and others. What does your loved one, friend, or colleague offer freely—time, service, words, a hug, thoughtful little gifts or cards? Think about what really pleases them; recall the times their eyes lit up at your thoughtfulness. These are huge clues to discerning their love language.

Or you could just *ask*! "Hey, I am reading this book about creating great relationships and trying to learn some things I can do to improve ours. How do you most like me to show my love and appreciation to you?"

Love languages may seem like an odd term to use with respect to business, but it applies to every relationship. It's simply realizing everyone, including your customers, clients, and business associates, has a unique way they feel appreciated and express care. For example, if an executive assistant knows her boss values spending quality time with his clients, she can schedule his appointments accordingly with leeway for meetings running overtime. One entrepreneur I coached sends thank-you gifts to his clients and colleagues whose love language is gifts, but takes the time to call and speak affirmations and encouragement to those whose love language is words of affirmation.

Figuring out a person's love language is an ingenious way to start the adventure of really *learning them*. Once you discover it, practice using their specific language when you want to communicate your appreciation, care, or admiration.

Learning Them applies to every relationship as a way to build trust and strengthen bonds.

Become a Detective

Tip #2: Investigate, Discover, and Dicern.

Observe and study them. Listen to the clues they drop. Pay attention to their nonverbal messages. (*Skill #1: Listen* will come in handy here.)

Pull out your detective gear and *Learn people*. Notice their preferences, habits, and idiosyncrasies, then interact with them based on what you learn. Doing so will increase your connection and improve your relationship because we are drawn to and enjoy being with people who make us feel seen, known, and cared for. Think about these people in your life... Aren't you more open with them? Are they some of your favorite folks to spend time with? Do you find it easier to trust them and want to get to know them better as well?

One of my clients, Sally, used Skill #2: Learn Them to stop arguments and reduce tension in her marriage. When Sally's kids were little, they enjoyed frequent afternoon play dates with a good mom friend and her kiddos. Quite often, Sally would get caught up in the middle of the fun activities and spontaneously invite them to stay for dinner. She didn't want the fun to end. However, her husband, Joe, was coming home expecting a relatively quiet house and some semblance of order, planning to spend the evening with Sally and the kids. Walking into a play date turned party was unsettling and resulted in tension and arguments.

As Sally learned him, she realized Joe needed time to shift gears and prepare for the change in plans before he walked in the door. So if the play date was going to be extended into dinnertime, she would call Joe during his commute home and prepare him. Sally also learned to check in with Joe before she extended the invite. She could tell when he didn't have the energy for extra friends at dinner. So she simply ended the play date and settled things down before Joe got home. This simple skill of learning him saved them from tense moments during an already chaotic time of day. Joe felt appreciated and respected. 'Learning him' helped reduce sharp words and tension-filled evenings.

Don't Box Me In

Tip #3: Give them room to grow and change.

We tend to put people in boxes or categories, often developed during or shortly after our initial experiences and interactions with them or when we begin to go deeper in the relationship. As human beings, we are constantly impacted, shaped, and refined by our experiences. We grow and change. We must give our friends, loved ones, and even coworkers room to do so too.

We miss transformations and the opportunity for deeper relationships when we keep people locked into our boxes or categories.

> *"The shortest distance between*
> *two people is a story."*
> —*Patti Digh*

Our past and ongoing stories, relationships, and experiences influence, shape, and change us. Harsh or shaming words and/ or bullying can influence an outgoing person and make them retreat, becoming more shy and withdrawn. A betrayed wife loses confidence in her ability to read people and grows increasingly cautious; this change begins to impact other relationships as well.

Conversely, praise and acclaim can increase confidence and boldness, empowering us to speak up more, share ideas, and engage in debate. Success often breeds generosity. Education and information can change our ideas and opinions, and impact our actions.

Thriving, growing, enjoyable relationships allow for and encourage growth in one another. Sometimes we may be uncomfortable when a friend or loved one changes. We may even be tempted to dissuade them in order to maintain the status quo. Yet, we would want grace and understanding if we were the ones making changes, growing or evolving into our best selves.

My client Mary experienced resistance when she began to grow and change. She loved going out with her sorority sisters. For years, their idea of fun and connection was an evening at the wine bar sharing stories, advice, and laughter. Over time, Mary realized she often had one too many glasses of wine; she felt out of control and wanted to change. She no longer relished her role as the "life of the party," and through our coaching work, she made some significant changes in her mindset and lifestyle.

As Mary grew, she became more subdued at their get-togethers. Mary believed her friends had put her in "the party girl" box and because of this seemed resistant to the changes she was making. When she was more restrained or turned down another glass of wine, they asked her what was wrong. Finally, Mary decided to be vulnerable with them. She shared her journey and the changes she was making. Was this risky? Absolutely. Mary was uncertain her friends would accept her and continue to include her. And if they did, would they pressure her to be the party girl or would they encourage her growth and new choices?

It takes courage to grow and change. When we are learning those we care about, we have to make space and allowances for this part of their journey too.

We desire encouragement and acceptance from our friends and loved ones when we make positive changes in our lives. Who wants to be the same in our forties as we were in our twenties? (Except for the collagen and energy!) Time and experience bring maturity and wisdom, which refine us. Embracing and celebrating growth in others strengthens our relationships and deepens our connections.

Imagine If...

- Imagine you have a weight-loss goal and significantly alter your eating habits. At the next family gathering, your well-meaning sister bakes your favorite cookies and presents them with an expectation you eat some... right now! Bummer! A lose-lose choice: compromise your goal or disappoint your sister. But what if, knowing about your goal, she had researched recipes, in line with your eating plan, and baked a treat based on your favorite flavors?
- What if a colleague knew you were pursuing advanced certification for a specific work issue and

when a new project arose, he assigned it to you, without you having to request it?

- What if your spouse, knowing you get caught up in a project and totally lose track of time, decided that instead of getting frustrated with you, he would give you a 15-minute heads up and then a five-minute warning before the "stop now and get ready" buzzer? Then... he put a cute timer in your Christmas stocking! (*True story.*)

- Imagine your activity-oriented friend is coming to visit. She is always in motion, with places to go, sights to see. Knowing this, you plan a jam-packed itinerary. But the day after she arrives, you feel lousy. Over morning coffee, she takes a good look at you, picks up your fun-filled, activity-packed itinerary, pulls out a pen and starts scratching things off. She says, "This is awesome and I really appreciate your efforts, but I am in the mood to be low-key and would love some time just to talk and hang out" (not wanting to point out that you are dragging). Or, she may just look at you, laugh, and say, "Are you kidding me? You look like death warmed over! Let's regroup and see how you feel as each day comes, but for now, how about a movie and some tea?"

Would you feel seen, known, and cared for? Would you be glad if the people in your life took the time to *learn you*? And—more importantly—how would your relationships improve if you *learned* the important people in your life and created opportunities for them to feel known and loved as well?

As you go on *Learn Them* treasure hunts, be sure to write down what you discover and learn about the people in your life. Memory fades, ink lasts, and today a smartphone makes note-taking easy. Harvey Mackay is famous for his Rolodex™ and the way he *learned* his clients. He was a master at *Learn Them*. Harvey kept meticulous notes about his friends, colleagues, and clients: their families, birthdays, and preferences. He used this information to communicate his care and investment in the relationship. His intentional relationship building yielded both personal and professional success. Being able to connect with people and build quality relationships is an invaluable skill.

Practicing *Learn Them* entails using *Listen* to help us pick up cues and hints about the likes, dislikes, and preferences of our loved ones, friends, and coworkers. You don't need three different pairs of glasses; intentionality and curiosity are better tools. We can observe, ask questions to provoke conversations, and go on treasure hunts to discover things below the surface. This information helps us personalize our expressions of care.

To dramatically improve your relationships, surprise the people in your life by communicating in their love language, creatively using the information you gather in *learning them* to make them feel special, cared about, and known.

They will love it!

Practicing *Listen, Learn, Love*

1. Think about your relationship avatars and apply *Learn Them*. Using your CSI super-sleuth skills, consider what

you know about them on a below-the-surface level... their moods, their hopes, dreams, hurts, or disappointments. Think of two specific things you can do to *learn them* more deeply. Write them down. Plan how and when you will put *Learn Them* into action this week.

2. Pick another relationship (spouse, kids, friends, family, or coworker) and surprise them in a way that communicates that you *learned them*. Be creative and clever! Did any person or ideas come to mind while you read? Look at your notes. If you have a number of people, make a list and choose one to focus on each day this week, or choose one individual each a week this month.

3. Make a list of your five most important and intimate relationships. Try to figure out their love languages, write them down, and use this information to improve your relationships. If you aren't sure about their love language, observe them or ask them.

4. Grab your sticky notes and write a *Learn Them* tip you want to put into action. Make two or three more sticky notes of the same tip and put them in strategic places to see throughout your day.

Please share how practicing and implementing these skills impacted your relationships on our Listen, Learn, Love Community page at www.ListenLearnLoveCommunity.com/stories.

Chapter 5

The Deeper Yes

"There is a time for risky love.
There is a time for extravagant gestures.
There is a time to pour out your affections
on the one you love. And when the time comes—
Seize it. Don't miss it."
—Max Lucado

Skill #3: Love Well

I realize this may sound like a strange term. You might be thinking, "Isn't love enough? What on earth does it mean to *Love Well*?" Bear with me as we unpack this term and see what you think at the end of this chapter.

Skill #3: Love Well is about sacrificial engagement. It is simply putting the needs of the other person in the relationship above your own. *Love Well* requires short-term sacrifice for long-term gain. It is often the opposite of "That was easy." *Loving Well* may be satisfying, but it is seldom effortless or our first instinct. I don't say this to scare you off, but to frame

95

Love Well differently from what often comes to mind when we hear the word "love". Sadly, it can conjure up cheesy prose on greeting cards, thirty-minute resolutions on sitcoms, or memories of your worst Valentine's Day.

Wouldn't you agree the word "love" is overused? At times we throw it around casually and with little thought. We say, "I love you" to the most important people in our lives and then cheapen the word by saying, "I love your new hairdo, outfit, or car." I often say it about a fabulous pair of shoes. Is it really the same? (Okay, I admit it is pretty close when it comes to shoes, but do I really love them as much as my spouse? Nope.) These lesser loves don't even come close to the same depth of meaning and value as loving another person in a committed relationship. *Love Well* is not casual. It requires commitment and choice.

Some languages have numerous words for the concept of love, each with a nuanced meaning. For example, the classical Greek language has three different words for three different types of love:

- *Philia*—Brotherly love: the fun comradery, enjoyment, and friendship kind of love.
- *Eros*—Love that implies passion, romance, and sexual intimacy.
- *Agape*—Sacrificial love, often used to describe the love of God, a deity, or a higher power.

Agape, or sacrificial love, captures the nuances of *Skill #3: Love Well.*

Whatever you view as your higher power, wouldn't you agree we need some divine intervention or assistance to help us *love well?* I rely on my relationship with God to help me engage sacrificially and *love well,* especially when relationships are difficult. On our own we can do the easy stuff and even a little bit of the hard stuff. We will compromise, be inconvenienced, and even uncomfortable for the people we care about... to a point. But when it comes to biting our tongue, putting the other person first, and sacrificing our wants, needs, desires, and preferences, it usually requires divine intervention or assistance! Choosing to put another person first, even when it is uncomfortable, painful, or not preferred by us, is the foundation of *Love Well.*

Remember doodling hearts as a young girl? Or the first Valentine you bought as a boy for your first girlfriend? Hearts were enough back then. As an adult, we are wiser, savvier, and maybe even a bit more cynical or protective when it comes to sharing our hearts or risking love, but we can't get away from it. Love is a universal language, desire, and emotion. We long to be loved for who we are, and we desire to love others. If only it were that simple. But love is messy and painful as much as it is rich and glorious. Broken hearts, dashed hopes, disappointments, and pain are as much a part of love as feeling cherished, enjoyed, and chosen. Love is multifaceted, risky yet beautiful, and blissful. We want it. We fear it. We can't live without it. *Loving well* is a full-contact emotion, requiring us to go all in, risking vulnerability and commitment in order to have a lasting and positive impact on our relationships.

Loving Well is a game changer. It takes any relationship to a deeper level of connection because *Loving Well* is born of commitment and choice; kicking selfishness to the curb. It is any action, engagement or behavior intended to bless and/or benefit another person. *Loving Well* is focused on the long game. We are guided by our desire to bless a loved one, friend, or even coworker. *Love well* means we choose short-term sacrifice for long-term gain. I call it choosing the "deeper yes."

Love Well in Action

Loving Well is exemplified in a mother's love for her child. Few things on earth compare to this kind of sacrificial love. Think about it. A mother's love begins as she gives up her body to nurture and grow her baby, carrying it to the time of birth—called labor for a reason! Followed by sleepless nights of care, feeding, diapers, prayer, dragging herself out of bed when her baby, toddler, tween, and even teen is sick.

Years of raising her children, teaching them, picking up after them, brushing teeth, doing laundry, loving on them, snuggling when she just wants to be left alone... dog-tired and weary. Countless hours of reading books, doing homework, school projects, making lunches, carpools, doing more laundry, and praying they will be safe... then doing it over and over again.

Moms do it because we love our kids, not for gratitude or accolades, but from a place of genuine, unreasonable, sacrificial—heart walking around outside your body—kind of love.

If you want a quick understanding of *Love Well*, spend some time with a mom. This skill requires consciously choosing to put another person's wants, desires, or interests above our own without any expectation of reward, repayment, or recognition.

> *"There is greatness in doing something*
> *you hate for the sake of someone you love."*
> —Rabbi Shmuley Boteach

Have you ever been the recipient of this kind of sacrificial love? Think about it… Picture yourself in the moment and recall the feelings of connection, safety, delight… a glimpse of heaven! I want to experience more of those moments… Don't you? And I want to give more amazing *Love Well* moments to the people in my life. I imagine you do, too.

That is the ideal.

While we aim for ideal, we live in reality.

We want to *Love Well*, and we hope others will do the same for us. But if we are brutally honest, most of us are in relationships where we are not often the giver or receiver of *Love Well*. We are just getting by as best we can.

Have you ever been in a relationship where you are always the giver? The one who compromises, understands, and just continually sucks it up, bites your tongue, and goes along? Have you ever felt taken advantage of or unappreciated in your marriage, family, or friendships? My guess is we all could answer "yes"; we have all experienced a time when we were not *loved well.*

Imagine If...

- Your spouse acknowledged your feelings of being unsupported in your parenting. Then during the next tense moment with the kids, they instructed them to stop arguing with you, do what you told them, and speak to you with respect?
- A sibling, who doesn't assist with caring for aging parents, heard the weariness in your voice, picked up some daily duties, and participated in hard conversations and decision-making details. What if they apologized for letting you shoulder all the responsibilities?
- One of your friends realized they were taking advantage of your willingness to help and began to give back, offering to drive extra car pools, have the kids at her house, or pick up the tab for lunch?

Looking Inward

In each of these vignettes, there was change—a choice to *Love Well.* If you were the recipient, would you feel seen, known, and cared for? Would you feel *loved well*?

Absolutely! Of course! Wouldn't that be totally awesome and incredible?!

Take a few minutes and write down a few folks and specific actions that came to mind while you were reading these examples. Who has shown you what it means to *Love Well*? Savor the memories and feelings of times you were *loved well.*

Now shift and think about the people and times you have chosen *to Love Well.* Be willing to acknowledge your good choices, the times you *Loved Well.* I imagine this brought gratifying feelings. *Loving Well* has its own unique benefits.

Let's also be honest about our need to grow and ask for some divine intervention to help us *Love Well.* Take a few moments to pause a bit longer and evaluate where you need to be the one to make the choice to *Love Well* in your relationships.

Love Well Applies to All Types of Relationships

Practicing *Listen, Learn, Love* will dramatically improve your personal and professional relationships. In *Listen* and *Learn Them,* we discussed how to specifically apply these skills not only with your loved ones and friends, but also to colleagues, coworkers, and clients.

Loving Well may sound like an odd concept to apply to the arena of work, business, clients, and customers. However, relationships are crucial to success in any business endeavor, and *Loving Well* is a posture of engagement that benefits the other. While this may be an uncommon practice in most businesses today, successful businesses flourish, even in difficult economic times, by applying this principle of putting others first. Later in the chapter, I will share some examples to illustrate how *Love Well* is essential to creating and/or improving business relationships.

Loving Well utilizes both the skills: *Listen* and *Learn Them*, but it is first and foremost about our motivation and choices.

Love Well is Not:
- Keeping score of who sacrifices more.
- Using candy, flowers, or any other means to smooth things over and avoid addressing issues after a conflict.
- Giving in to another person's whims, especially when it is unbeneficial to them.
- Looking the other way when a coworker is dishonest or acts in a manner detrimental to the business.
- Compromising your standards or acting against your morality or ethics.

Consider this classic example of not *Loving Well*: A parent gives in because their child is having a "come apart" and the parent is too tired, harried, or ill equipped to deal with it. We have all seen it happen. (You may have done it; I know I have!) We sigh, say "fine," and give in because we just want our child to be quiet, to stop arguing, and give us a break. (Thank goodness my kids are all grown up now!) Compare that to the following example of *Loving Well*.

Joey was an energetic six-year-old who, after a long day at the company picnic, begged his parents to let him stay up with the big kids. When his parents said, "No, it's time for bed," Joey pitched a fit and yelled at them for being mean, shouting, "It's not fair! You never say 'yes!'" This kind of outburst is hard enough to handle in the privacy of your own home, but it's exponentially worse at the company picnic with your boss and coworkers as witnesses!

Giving in and letting Joey stay up would be far easier. However, it would not be loving well. Joey's parents were clients and had been practicing the skills of learning him. They knew Joey's tantrums usually occurred when he was utterly exhausted. They realized Joey was too young to rein himself in and stop his outburst. Developmentally, he was unable to ask for what he really needed, sleep.

Through our work together, their confidence increased both in their ability to say "No" and to stick to their plan. Learning Joey and Loving Well meant saying "no" and putting him to bed. So, at the picnic, Joey's parents didn't waver. Did they cringe and hope no one actually witnessed Joey's tantrum? Sure. Were they tempted to give in? Absolutely! But they chose to Love Well. They stayed the course; they picked up Joey, carried him to their hotel room, and put him to bed.

Was it fun? No. Hard? Yes. But, worth it to have a well-rested son the next day, not to mention the respect of their coworkers for having the guts to parent well by loving well.

Love Well Is:

- Putting your knowledge about the important people in your life into action with the intention of blessing or benefiting them.

- Acting on behalf of and in the best interests of the other, especially when you least feel like it.
- Valuing the relationship more than your comfort, convenience, or emotions.

We all like the concept of loving and being loved. But *Loving Well* requires sacrifice, consciously choosing to put the other person's needs and wants first. It is saying "no" to me and "yes" to you, borne of our desire to be a blessing or support—to be a giver in our relationships—especially when it means being uncomfortable, disappointed, or doing without something we want.

I see incredible examples of *Loving Well* quite often in my private coaching practice. One of my favorites is when I have been working with a woman and she has braved the conversation of saying to her spouse, "We need to get some counseling/marriage coaching together." Rarely, if ever, does the spouse reply, "Absolutely, I totally agree and am so glad you brought that up!" More often than not, they are shocked, defensive, and resistant.

Isabella was a brave woman who chose to love her husband well. She hated conflict and, while she wanted more from her marriage to Mike, she didn't really want to have the uncomfortable and potentially conflictual conversation about getting marriage coaching. Mike had mentioned to Isabella that she seemed distant. Isabella kept blaming it on work pressures and hassles with the kids, but she knew that wasn't the whole truth.

Isabella and I worked on how she would approach Mike about getting marriage coaching. We discussed what words to say and how to handle any objections he might have. Even though she was anxious and would have preferred avoidance, Isabella chose to Love Well and have the hard conversation.

Mike told me later he was concerned about the tension between them, but he hoped it would just get better. He admitted his hesitancy to discuss their problems with a stranger, but he wanted a better relationship with Isabella. He missed the intimacy and fun of their early years. Mike agreed to marriage coaching so he and Isabella could build a mutually fulfilling relationship. After three weeks of practicing Listen, Learn, Love, Mike said to me, "Susie, I was skeptical, but these skills work! We had the best conversation last night!" We continued to work together and they went through one of my coaching programs to create a deeper connection through learning the Five Kinds of Intimacy. They are back to having fun, have crafted a remarkable relationship, and no longer avoid discussing difficult issues... In this scenario, both Isabella and Mike chose to Love Well. They both put the other's needs and desires above their own.

Tips to Practice Skill #3: Love Well

Loving Well is the most nuanced of the three skills. It draws on both *Listen* and *Learn Them*. Through the process of discovery, using the first two skills, you will gain information and insight about the important people in your life, which you can apply in creative ways to *Love Well*. Let's unpack this skill further and equip you with some tips and tools to practice and bring about positive shifts in your relationships. While *Loving Well* may be challenging, it is always worth it!

> *"Being deeply loved by someone gives you strength,*
> *while loving someone deeply gives you courage."*
> —Lao Tzu

Pitfalls and Potholes

Tip #1: Awareness of what will get in your way.

"Love well" are action words implying effort and intentionality. To *Love Well*, we must be acutely aware of the pitfalls and potholes that can trip us up or steer us off course. It is crucial to know how our moods, frustrations, stress, and fatigue impact our decisions. And we must be honest about the thoughts, beliefs, and fears that may get in our way and stop us from choosing to *Love Well*.

The Smiths were a power couple. Mr. Smith was a successful entrepreneur; Mrs. Smith was a lawyer. Their three kids were active in sports, successful in school, and popular with their peers. The whole family was involved in their local church and community. The Smiths had a reputation of being "the perfect family." However, behind closed doors things were crumbling. Their teenage daughter had been drinking for a year and her behavior was getting out of control. After trying numerous treatment options, her doctor recommended they admit her to an inpatient program for teenage alcohol addiction. Fear, disagreements, and fights erupted in the Smiths' relationship, and they hired me for marriage coaching.

While they were grateful to get out from under the pressure of maintaining the façade of being the perfect family, it was difficult to acknowledge the full truth and stark reality of their situation. Admitting their daughter had an addiction and needed to literally "get away" from them in order to get better broke their hearts. Facing reality, and taking this difficult and very public action, was not only gut-wrenching, but also tugged at their "what will people think" strings.

(For all our independence and self-confidence, let's be honest and acknowledge that at one time or another we have all thought, "What will people think?" Full disclosure: This fear has tripped me up. I can recall numerous times when I needed to remind myself that another's perception of me ultimately doesn't matter. It was an exercise in clinging to the truth so I could get out of my own way, make the best decision, and take action, regardless of what anyone else might think.)

Back to the Smiths. Fear of other people's opinions could have stopped them from making the difficult decision for their daughter. They could have lived in denial or talked themselves into trying another local counselor in order to keep up appearances. They knew the neighborhood gossip mill might not be kind, but they chose to Love Well and admitted their daughter for treatment. She got the necessary help and recovered. The Smiths built a strong marriage and their family is resilient. Their dark days of grief and struggle eventually led to a sense of freedom. They no longer feel pressure to be the perfect family. The Smiths enjoy authentic and delightful relationships with one another and their kids. Today they encourage and work with other families who are struggling with similar issues.

It takes courage to acknowledge what could stop us from making the hard decision to say "the deeper yes," in choosing to *Love Well*. Sometimes, I don't want to admit it is a choice. I want to ignore or deny responsibility. Blaming someone or something else is easier, but doing so isn't healthy, honest, or beneficial for any relationship. *Loving Well* involves examining our motivations and making intentional choices; sometimes it's harder than we ever imagined.

Another example of being aware of what could trip us up from *Loving Well* happened with some clients who live in the South, where manners and customs are particularly important. I was working with a mom and her adult daughter whose relationship had begun to level out after weathering some storms. They were enjoying each other and getting along. The daughter, Amy, is a bright and independent twenty-something who challenges conventions and needs to understand "the why" before complying with rules. Her mom, Sarah, is talented, smart, and a peacemaker.

Amy is a classic Millennial who challenges convention. Her independence and tendency to question authority can get in her way and prevent her from loving well. A simple conversation about manners at the dinner table escalated into an argument. The issue: elbows on the table. Amy thinks etiquette rules are ridiculous and old-fashioned, and sees little value in them. Amy blew up at her mom because whenever they sit next to each other at the table, Sarah will push Amy's elbows off the table. Amy believes, as an adult, she should be able to do whatever she wants, even in her mom's home.

Amy argued, "I don't know why it is such a big deal that I put my elbows on the table! Sometimes I am just being comfortable and other times, I just do it inadvertently."

Softly, Sarah said, "It might not be a big deal to you, but it is to me because when you sit with your elbows on the table I feel like I didn't do a good job raising you."

I said to Amy, "I know you think 'no elbows on the table' is a dumb rule and shouldn't be a big deal to your mom. But did you hear what she said about why it is important to her?" Amy nodded.

I continued, "So whether or not it makes sense to you, wouldn't it be kind to your mom if you made the effort to keep your elbows off the table? Wouldn't that be a way of loving her well?" Reality dawned on Amy... It wasn't about the rule; it was about respect. Amy realized she had let her personal view of etiquette rules and her fierce independence get in the way of loving well.

Two drastically different examples, but both required awareness of how our beliefs, fear, attitudes, or opinions can get in our way and stop us from choosing to *Love Well*. In big moments and small gestures, *loving well* goes a long way toward forming strong relationships.

Stress: work, financial, relational, or situational can impact our ability to *Love Well*. When these pressures are beyond our control we need to step back and not engage in sensitive or highly charged issues until we have a bit more margin in our lives, minds, and hearts.

Health challenges and worries can impact our ability to be attentive to another person's needs in a given moment or time frame. During these seasons it is important to be honest with yourself, your loved ones, and friends and ask for what you need. Take care of yourself, get some space, and recharge enough to be able to reenter with some energy and engagement geared toward blessing others.

I can address one last example, because I am female. Sometimes, women can be more sensitive or have a tendency to have a short fuse—just every so often—about once a month, in fact! All humor aside, ladies… let's be honest about our hormones and how they affect us. It's better to warn our families up front: "This week, talk to the hand!"

Being aware and honest about what may prevent us from *Loving Well* is a big step in practicing this skill.

Short-term Sacrifice for Long-term Gain

Tip #2: Be willing to sacrifice.

Sacrifice, by definition, means putting someone else's needs, wants, desires above our own. It means we are willing to take the blame, be misunderstood, judged, inconvenienced, disappointed and/or bear another's burden.

In the movie *Stepmom*, Jackie, a divorced mom, is put in a difficult position when her ex-husband, Luke, asks her to help break the news to their kids that he is getting remarried. The conversation promises to be difficult because their daughter, Anna, dislikes his fiancé, Isabel, and both she and her brother Ben still hold out hope that their parents will reunite. Isabel is struggling to connect with the kids and marrying their dad will make that even harder.

Luke not only enlists Jackie's help to tell the kids; he also asks her to help make the transition easier. Jackie has no reason to agree. She is justifiably angry, as the dutiful wife whose ex-husband is now marrying a younger woman. However, for the sake of Anna and Ben, Jackie agrees to help Luke.

Upon hearing the engagement announcement, Anna and Ben are fuming, disappointed, and hurt. Jackie takes their hands, calms theirs fears, makes positive comments about Isabel, and reasons this marriage will benefit the kids. Jackie *loves well.*

Loving well is challenging, especially when it is costly. Making the choice to *Love Well* is even more fulfilling and meaningful in these moments.

My husband, John, dreamed of being a millionaire by age 30. This was not a pipe dream as he was raised in an entrepreneurial family, started his own business at age 19, and was following in the footsteps of his already successful brother. I remember our conversation a few weeks after John's 30th birthday. He was struggling because he had not achieved his entrepreneurial dream. I listened and reminded him of the reason his dream was delayed.

When our kids were young, John chose to be an involved dad. He delighted in our kids and enjoyed spending time with them. When they started playing sports, he decided to be actively involved in coaching them as well. Parenting well requires time and energy; coaching also involves a significant time commitment. John sacrificed his entrepreneurial dream to invest in our kids. He willingly gave up one dream to fulfill another—to be an engaged dad and build strong relationships with his kids. The reward he enjoys today is far more valuable than money or status. He created a unique and amazing relationship with each of our children, which continued as they became adults. John made sacrifices and difficult choices as an entrepreneur, but he truly believes that he chose "'the deeper yes.'"

Loving Well can dramatically improve your relationships. Think about a time when you were on the receiving end of someone sacrificing for your benefit. How did it feel? (Pretty amazing, huh?)

A remarkable thing about *Love Well* is that we get those same awesome feelings when we choose to *Love Well* or sacrifice for another! Remember, your sacrifice isn't in vain, even if it goes unrecognized or appreciated. Again, look at any mother and ask her if she keeps a tally sheet of all she does. *Loving Well* doesn't keep score or expect payment in return.

*"When you love you wish to do things for,
you wish to sacrifice for, you wish to serve."*
—Ernest Hemingway

Skill #3: Love Well is not often our first instinct as the world warns us to look out for number one and protect ourselves from being taken advantage of, and cautions against being a doormat. Conversely, *Loving Well* sacrifices and gives for the benefit of others, embracing an abundance mentality knowing that in giving, we receive; in blessing others we are blessed. *Loving Well* believes generosity and sacrifice have their own rewards.

Driven by Our Commitments

Tip #3: Loving Well is based on commitment, not emotions.
Sometimes we won't feel like being sacrificial. It is hard, uncomfortable, and simply not what we want to do sometimes. *Loving Well* does not require us to "feel like it"—but rather to make a conscious choice to act according to our commitments and not be governed by our emotions. *Loving Well* means choosing to do it anyway.

For example, there are days when we don't always feel like working on our business, making the next sales call, pushing through rejection, or getting up early for massive action, but successful entrepreneurs and business executives do it anyway; they work from their commitments, not their emotions.

As parents, we are rarely eager to leave our warm beds to get our kids ready for school, give them a nutritious breakfast, and pack lunches to save money for the family vacation, but we do it anyway.

On evenings when we are dog-tired, the last thing we have energy for is a long conversation with our teenager who had a hard day at school. But we patiently listen, validating, and clarifying, with toothpicks holding our eyes open. Sometimes we are angry and frustrated and, instead of being understanding, we want to snap at our spouse and tell them exactly how we think they should handle a sticky situation at work. Instead, we remember our commitment to allow them to "just vent," so we bite our tongue and patiently listen as they recount a frustrating or challenging work issue.

Maybe a friend requested your help holding her accountable in an area in which she wanted to grow and change: boundaries, diet, exercise, time management. She is frustrated, discouraged, and compromised her plan, but saying something is harder than pretending not to notice. Besides, you don't want to make her mad and add to her struggles. *Loving well* in this case means braving the hard conversation.

In each of these situations we can choose to *Love Well* by acting from our commitments, not from our emotions. I know this is hard to do. We are emotionally driven beings, and it takes practice and discipline to manage our emotional response, and choose to act from our decisions made in rational moments.

We cannot control *how* we feel, but we can control *what* we do with our feelings. Sacrifice and putting the needs of others first is easier when we are "feeling it." However, we can choose to intentionally engage for another's benefit, especially when we are dog-tired, inconvenienced, uncomfortable, or just plain uninterested. In these moments, when we put our emotions aside and honor our relational commitments, we are *loving well.*

My client Walter was a stressed-out, time-constrained, successful C-level executive, who needed more hours in every day. With four kids, he had attended countless band concerts, baseball games, ballets, and school assemblies through the years. He shared honestly that he didn't want to attend these anymore; it felt like a waste of his time, especially since they started to sound and look the same... except for the people involved. When his third child, Jake, was the one up at bat, on stage, getting an award or warming the bench, Walter's presence mattered, especially to his son. Loving Well meant Walter set an alarm on his phone, promptly left work, breezing by, and disappointing the colleagues who followed him down the hall saying, "This will just take a minute," grabbed a quick dinner, and trekked to Jake's school or activity—choosing to be present and engaged even when it is was the last thing he preferred to do with his evening.

Love Well in Business

I mentioned earlier that *Loving Well* might seem like an unusual term to use in the business world. However, I believe it's totally applicable. I am convinced more businesses, salespeople, and executives would enjoy greater success if they intentionally employed *Listen, Learn, Love* in their professional relationships.

> *"Your true worth is determined by how much more*
> *you give in value than you take in payment."*
> —Bob Burg

Are you wondering what exactly *Love Well* would look like applied to the business and entrepreneurial world or in relationships with clients and customers? A great place to start is with the book, *The Go Giver: A Little Story about a Powerful Business Idea,* by Bob Burg and John David Mann, which focuses on a giving mindset specifically applied to the workplace. It is a great story about an ambitious businessman named Joe, who learns how changing his focus, from getting to giving, and putting the interests of others before his own ultimately leads to unexpected rewards.

If you want to practice *Love Well* in your professional relationships, keep the following questions at the forefront of all your interactions: How can I give to the other person in this relationship? How can I add value to my client, my customer, and my colleague rather than have a quid pro quo attitude? How can I show appreciation and gratitude for my client, colleague, or customer?

Using *Love Well* as an entrepreneur may mean telling a client you are not the best one to meet their needs and referring them to a competitor. Do you think this client will ever forget that you put their interests above your profit? Can you imagine how they will tell the story to their friends? You can't pay for that kind of good will and word-of-mouth advertising.

You may advise a new client to choose a lower-priced package of your product or service because it's a better match for their budget, even though you're trying to meet a sales goal. You gain their trust by demonstrating you have their best interests at heart. Trust and integrity are invaluable commodities in business. *Loving Well* at work may mean engaging in a hard conversation with an employee or coworker about a problem or unsatisfactory work because a good team environment and greater productivity are more important than our discomfort with difficult discussions.

With my coaching clients, *Love Well* sometimes looks like "tough love" or saying hard things, rather than easy and more palatable ones. Do my clients respond with, "Thanks for saying that?" Rarely. But they know I am *for them* and willing to incur their anger or handle their push back for the purpose of their growth. This builds trust and deepens our connection. Can you see how *Love Well* is an essential skill to succeed in your professional relationships?

The Big-Picture Skill

Any time we choose to put the needs and interests of someone else above our own, we are *Loving Well*. This is a big-picture skill. An "I'm in this for the long haul" relationship posture. *Loving Well* isn't easy; it doesn't come naturally, but it is a valuable skill, an intentional choice that will significantly impact the quality of our relationships.

"What a grand thing, to be loved!
What a grander thing still, to love!"
—Victor Hugo

Picture yourself as the wife whose husband chose to skip watching the game to put the kids to bed so you could enjoy an evening with your girlfriends. After uncorking the wine, heating up the snacks, your hubby kissed you and said, "I've got this... Just pretend you don't hear us upstairs and have fun with your friends." Would that feel awesome? Would you feel *loved well*?

During one of my events, one of the attendees, Elizabeth, left abruptly after receiving a call informing her that a dear friend's father had suddenly passed away. Elizabeth had invested time and money to be part of this training, and there was no guarantee she would recoup it. But none of that mattered.

Elizabeth's friend needed her. On a moment's notice, without hesitation, Elizabeth changed her plans, left the weekend event, and traveled home because she wanted to be there for her grieving friend. This is Loving Well. (We did arrange for a refund and a reserved spot for her in the next one.)

Wouldn't it be comforting if, in the midst of a difficult time, a dear friend dropped everything to be with you? You need her; she is there—tissues, stories or silent support—depending on what is best for you in the moment. Would you feel *Loved Well?*

What if... You stood your ground the next time your teenager is frustrated with you because—well, because she is a

teenager! Pick a reason: You refused to let her go to a party...
You made her change an outfit you deemed inappropriate...
You limited her cell-phone use... censored a movie choice.

She is mad because you said "No."

And in spite of a very loud barrage of: "You don't
understand!" "It's *not* fair!" "You're a prude" "I hate you!" and
"I'm never doing this to my kids!"—there you are still standing
your ground.

Picture that moment... Wouldn't it be amazing to feel
confident in your parenting choices, and gratified because
you don't need your kids to like or approve of your decisions?
After all, you aren't out to be their friend; you are their parent!
You don't need them to like you. (It would be nice, but not a
necessity when it comes to good parenting or *Loving Well*.)

You choose to *Love Well* because you are willing to incur
their wrath and stand your ground. Sure, you may need some
reinforcement from your spouse, a good friend, your mom, or
a large glass of wine... but hang in there because you did the
right thing! Was it hard? Yes! But does it feel good! Yes! *Loving
Well* feels great because ultimately it is the right thing to do!

What if... the next time you and your spouse are in an
argument, instead of retorting with sharp words of debate or a
laundry list of things you do to anger or frustrate him, your spouse
pauses? Silence. He looks at you and says, "I'm sorry... You are
right. I have been too busy and totally preoccupied with work. I
have blown off my commitments to be home for dinner and have
cancelled our date nights. I have taken you for granted."

Would you feel *Loved Well*? Would the whole tenor of the argument change? Maybe even turning it from an argument into a discussion as your defenses drop and together you talk about how it got to this point? Suddenly, you aren't quite as mad, and you're able to share your sadness and how much you miss him. *Loving Well* changes conversations, people, and relationships.

Learning and practicing *Love Well* can dramatically improve your relationships—even if you are the only one making this choice. We are emotional beings and respond to people sacrificing on our behalf, so give it time; don't give up; keep *Loving Well*. Eventually, the tide will turn and you can enjoy learning and growing together.

Loving Well builds an unshakable foundation when practiced by both people in a relationship.

It is the stuff long marriages are made of, where partners are connected and still enjoy each other 30 years later... having navigated the many stages of raising kids into productive adults who still like and respect you. It is also the stuff of long-term friendships that endure through challenges, changes, and different life paths... of lasting business partnerships that weather economic storms... and of strong family relationships that sometimes are akin to riding a roller coaster.

These are rich and valuable relationships because you have *loved well* and have been *loved well*.

Loving Well changes lives.

Relationships grow and thrive when we make the choice

to *Love Well* because trust grows, defenses come down, and we become more authentic and transparent, causing our relationships to reach deeper levels.

Every day we have countless opportunities to *Love Well*.

Practicing *Listen, Learn, Love*

1. Pick a relationship avatar; think back on an interaction in which you just wanted to have your own way and you breezed or bulldozed over their needs. Reimagine the scene with you making the choice to *Love Well*. Decide if you want to address it with them in person.

2. Recall a recent business exchange or client interaction that was more quid pro quo than go-give. How would you handle it differently using *Skill #3: Love Well*?

3. Think about the days and weeks ahead; ponder the potential interactions in your relationships. Try to envision and plan some conversations in which you can practice *Love Well*. Jot down a few notes for each one that comes to mind.

4. Choose a *Love Well* tip to focus on in the coming month. Write it on a sticky note and put it beside the others. (If you haven't done any sticky notes yet, write one tip for each skill on a single sticky; at least it's a start!) Of course, you should make three more of this same note to place on your bathroom mirror, steering wheel, TV remote or desk, so you have multiple reminders throughout the day!

5. As you read through the examples of *Love Well,* did anyone come to mind who had loved you well? Take a moment and send them a note, email, or text or pick up the phone and say "thank you."

6. Call your mom because she is definitely one person who loved you sacrificially!

Please share how practicing and implementing these skills impacted your relationships on our Listen, Learn, Love Community page at www.ListenLearnLoveCommunity.com/stories.

Chapter 6

Possibilities and Potential

*"To be fully seen by somebody then and
be loved anyhow—this is a human offering
that can border on miraculous."*
—Elizabeth Gilbert

Pause for a moment and think about the people in your life with whom you can really be yourself... authentic, uncensored, messy, grubby clothes, without makeup, struggling, transparent, doubtful... moments of discouragement, despair, anxiety, mania... your fears hanging out and even your flaws and idiosyncrasies showing.

Who has seen you at your worst and still knows you at your best, and who love, enjoys, and accepts you either way? Whom do you trust with the real you? If you can count these people on one hand, you are blessed. I would wager that with each of them, you have used all three skills to create a great relationship that allows for authenticity, without second-guessing the relationship. You share a security in knowing you are seen, known, and loved, not just in spite of who you are, but because of who you are!

However, most of our relationships fall along a spectrum of authenticity, intimacy, and connection. We have a myriad of relationships with different purposes, levels of involvement, and commitment. This is totally normal! We have spouses, kids, siblings, parents, friends, family, colleagues, partners, clients, and customers, to name a few categories. And in most of these categories we have multiple relationships with different levels of connection. Some are going well; some are great! Some are tension-filled, difficult, or mediocre. No matter what, they all could get better!

Regardless of where they fall on the spectrum, we can improve our personal and professional relationships using *Listen, Learn, Love.*

Quick Results *and* Long-Lasting Changes

Warning #1: Long-term and regular use of *Listen, Learn, Love* will result in authentic and rewarding relationships!

Quick results come when you begin to use these skills in your relationships. As you pause to *listen* and pay attention when talking with your spouse, friend, or teen, they may notice your increased engagement and let down their guard, and share more of their thoughts and feelings. (Your relationship just improved!)

Recently, I heard from a client whose husband had learned her love language as a result of a conversation they had about *learn them*. He brought her a chocolate treat along with the regular groceries she asked him to pick up. This deposit in her love bank made her feel cared about and came as delightful surprise at the end of a long day. (Their relationship just improved.)

Relationship changes are a bit like a sand timer; sometimes the grains get stuck in the middle. Clogged, static, with no movement, it ceases to be effective as a sand timer. But give it a little shake, the pieces begin to "get unstuck" and shift. Suddenly, whoosh, a whole bunch of grains flow through to the other side.

Our relationships are similar—A few shifts can yield rapid and significant improvement. Long-term results come from using these skills over and over again—Not giving up when it gets hard and employing them on a regular basis. Learning and practicing *Listen, Learn, Love* is the first step to creating *better* relationships. Going deeper and mastering these skills requires a longer book specifically tailored to different relationships. This book offers a broad brushstroke of these skills and how using them can improve your relationships. It is meant to give you results and *hope*.

As empty-nesters, my hubby and I are enjoying this time of life and the benefits of learning and practicing these fundamental skills over the course of our marriage. Do we always get it right? Heck no! Being married to a serial entrepreneur is challenging. So is being married to me! However, after years of practice, we return to these skills more quickly than we did in our younger years when we blew it and made a mess of things... a lot!

Love Well practiced repeatedly, even with missteps and moments of utter selfishness, will yield lasting results if you don't give up. Our marriage wasn't always wonderful or even easy. Some years it was incredibly hard... and a few times, I wasn't sure we would make it. We had some difficult seasons and have endured some serious trials and life-altering events, which, statistically, should have destroyed our marriage. But, we are stubborn and our faith carried us through the toughest times and darkest days. Today, we are thriving and our relationship is rich and rewarding. It was worth the hard work of learning and practicing these three essential skills... over and over again. As we have gotten older and wiser, we remember the crucial question: *Is being right more important than this relationship?* I share this not to brag but to give you hope.

These skills work! I have seen this with countless clients as well as in my own life. Practicing and using *Listen, Learn, Love* will dramatically improve your relationships... quickly! You will see improvements in the short term as well as build long-term results for strong, rich, and rewarding relationships. So no matter what condition your relationships are in, don't give up until you give these skills a try. You can make a difference in every relationship if you are willing to be intentional and make an effort.

Life is good when our relationships are thriving... Love, family, friends, and career are all in sync.

Listen, Learn, Love at Work

A few thoughts about *Listen, Learn, Love* at work. If your personal relationships were easier, more comfortable, and fulfilling, would you be less stressed, more patient, and enjoyable? And would that shift have a positive impact on your effectiveness at work? All combined, can you see how better personal and professional relationships would enhance your quality of life?

A successful entrepreneur struggled to build a cohesive support team and didn't understand why he couldn't keep a virtual assistant long-term. As we looked at the way he engaged in conversations, we discovered he needed to use these skills to better communicate his expectations, as well as show appreciation for their efforts and a job well done. After two weeks of practicing Listen, Learn, Love *his team noticed a difference! Now he enjoys longevity and loyalty with his support team, which resulted in lower stress levels and increased profitability.*

Relationships are the currency of today and essential for success in life and in business. When our personal relationships are going well, we have energy to devote to our entrepreneurial endeavors and professional relationships without being stressed about personal issues.

People who develop positive professional relationships enjoy greater success through faster promotions, increased sales, and more clients because we are drawn to people who make us feel good. We are not moved by statistics, facts, or figures; we are moved by emotions. We do business with people we know, like, and trust. These three simple, elegant, and effective skills will equip you to develop strong and thriving relationships, thereby increasing your effectiveness and profitability.

When studying successful and long-lasting business partnerships, like Ben Cohen and Jerry Greenfield, Bill Gates and Paul Allen, Bill Hewlett and Dave Packard, I discovered that not only did they share similar passions and interests, but in every case, they were also friends. Their business partnerships were built on a solid relationship that lasted through the years.

Time and again, I have seen how our personal and professional relationships intertwine, overlap, and impact each other.

"Succeed at home, and all
other relationships become easier."
—John Maxwell

Relationship Realities

Thriving and satisfying relationships simply make life better. However, in reality, for many of us, our relationships are mediocre, tense, or just plain boring.

We muddle through...

On the worst days, we have felt the sting of a relationship in jeopardy... are devastated by the pain of one that is lost... or discouraged and weary from the burden of a tension-filled relationship.

On the best days, we have glimpses of connection with the soulmate we longed for... the teen who is happy... the friend who just "gets" us and we experience a bond that gives us hope for the future of our relationship. Or perhaps our spirits soar with excitement about new business growth.

In these moments, we experience the connection we are hardwired for and enjoy the wonder of life-giving relationships.

We have hope.

A smile lights up our face after a delightful and meaningful conversation with our spouse. Feelings of satisfaction and affirmation stem from words of appreciation and a hug from our college-aged kid. We enjoy a deep sense of belonging with good friends who really know and enjoy us. There is a bounce in our step because a client finally pulled the trigger and signed the contract due to the relationship we invested in and developed over time.

These are times when *life is good*. That's why we risk, try, and invest in relationships. We long to know and to be known. We are eternal optimists... hoping this time our risk will be rewarded.

Relationships are the stuff of life. We can't avoid them or

exist without them. So doesn't it make sense to learn how to create and sustain good—if not great—ones?

I bet you can think of at least one relationship you want to *be better.* These skills will help! If you learn and practice them, your relationships will become more fulfilling, productive, and just plain old more fun! Mastering them will radically change your life. However, you can't do this with a transactional mentality. You need a relational mentality... because the basis of all great relationships is heart-driven. We pursue relationships because we desire to have a positive impact on the lives of others. We want to make a difference. We long to be connected.

> *"Nothing is perfect. Life is messy.*
> *Relationships are complex.*
> *Outcomes are uncertain. People are irrational."*
> —Hugh Mackay

Dare Greatly

Warning #2: You will make mistakes; it will be messy. (Don't panic!)

"Messy" isn't a bad word. "Messy" means you are engaged, invested, and committed. You have the courage to actually be in the arena trying... not standing on the sideline wishing and hoping things change or get better. (Hint: They won't— Wishing and hoping without action are ineffective strategies.)

"Messy" means you are making an effort.

The good news: Practicing these three skills will bring far more rewards than the effort you make. Why? Because we desperately desire to connect; thus, we are delighted when someone makes an effort on our behalf, whether or not they get it right!

So "messy" is worth it!

"Messy" at least means you are invested, wanting more, and willing to try!

As a young wife and mom, I battled fears and insecurities; I struggled with how to handle my mistakes with grace and acceptance. I sought counseling (it helped) along with inspiration, truth, and encouragement from the Bible. I also gathered words of wisdom and quotations. As a recovering perfectionist, one of my favorite quotations is about being willing to be in the arena: sweaty and tired from genuine, intentional effort; bloodied knees from failed attempts; bright, hope-filled eyes; daring to risk in order to create something worthwhile:

"It is not the critic who counts; not the man who points out how the strong man stumbles, or where the doer of deeds could have done them better. The credit belongs to the man who is actually in the arena, whose face is marred by dust and sweat and blood; who strives valiantly; who errs, who comes up short again and again, because there is no effort without error and shortcoming; but who does actually strive to do the deeds; who knows great enthusiasms, the great devotions; who spends himself in a worthy cause; who at the best knows in the end the triumph of high achievement, and who at the worst, if he fails, at least fails while daring greatly, so that his place shall never be with those cold and timid souls who neither know victory nor defeat."
—Theodore Roosevelt

These words still inspire and embolden me! What about you? Does reading them make you want to jump into the arena and try? (Even just a little?) Handwritten on an index card, splattered, and timeworn, those words lived on my refrigerator for years, reminding me to be courageous in trying and to be gentle with myself in making mistakes.

When I read Brene Brown's excellent book, *Daring Greatly: How the Courage to Be Vulnerable Transforms the Way We Live, Love, Parent, and Lead*, and learned her concept of *"daring greatly together,"* this quotation took on even more meaning! Brown teaches about having the courage to engage together in honest vulnerability to transform our lives and relationships.

I love her concept of *daring greatly together* because it makes *Listen, Learn, Love* even more effective in the glorious mess of relationships. We can support, encourage, and champion each other as we try to succeed, as well as fail... only to try again.

Let's *dare greatly* together! I promise it is worth the risk! You can be one of the brave ones who choose to invest yourself in the worthiest of causes: the people in your life! Real victory and results come by showing up, being in the trenches, and making an effort to improve your relationships. Doing so communicates more than you can imagine, because most people long to know they are worthy of your efforts, even clumsy, awkward, or messy ones!

I encourage you... even dare you to jump in. It's okay to be scared and feel awkward, and unsure. It's not okay to wimp out.

It takes more courage to take action when we are afraid and uncertain — I call it "jumping scared!" If we wait for 100% confidence, we will never jump. We will miss the thrill of trying and the wonder of exponential returns on our heartfelt efforts.

Let me take the pressure off and tell you up front—it's okay to mess up—In fact, you will blow it. Big time.

Daring greatly implies a learning curve. Jumping scared means we aren't 100% sure, but we are willing to engage. We won't allow the fear of messy relationships to hold us back. Relationships require risk and the end results aren't guaranteed. We will make mistakes.

But, rest assured, as you begin to practice, and then practice some more, you will get it right more often!

I have blown it, many times, over and over again! And "relationships" is what I teach, write, and speak about for a living. I am supposed to be "the expert." So take heart; growth is a process... a lifelong journey!

I have jumped scared and made huge messes. I have jumped scared and seen relationships improve and grow. I have an overflowing basket of stories collected from clients, friends, and family who have done the same. Their courage inspires me!

So take a deep breath and relax. You're in good company. Please be gracious and patient with yourself as you learn and practice *Listen, Learn, Love.* You will feel uncomfortable, inept, and maybe even silly. Remember these feelings usually come whenever we are brave enough to attempt new things! (So, if you are having them, you are probably being courageous and jumping scared!)

Yoda is Wrong

When you make mistakes, don't quit. Remember to say to yourself, "I am trying, and that will make a difference!" Improving your relationships comes through trying—taking action and making an effort!

The only way to fail at this is not to try.

Yoda is wrong. In relationships, there is *always try*! In fact, that is *how* you actually do relationships!

Life is messy.

Relationships are messy.

Authentic, meaningful, and long-term relationships are even messier.

The worst part of making a mess... you have to clean it up. (These skills will help.)

The best part of making a mess... you may create something more incredible than you ever imagined possible: loving, thriving, delightful, authentic, deeply connected relationships!

So have the courage to dare greatly, get messy, and try! Go ahead and jump scared!

Perfection isn't the goal. Practice is.

And remember: Practice doesn't make perfect—Practice means you're willing to try, to learn, and to grow. Practicing *Listen, Learn, Love* in your relationships communicates care, commitment, and a desire for connection. Continue to practice and, over time, you will get increasingly better at using each skill.

Practice Makes ~~Perfect~~ Comfortable

Building great relationships, both personally and professionally, doesn't have to be all consuming. It does take some time and intentionality, but not the massive action of an entrepreneurial start-up, the intensity of the honeymoon phase of a relationship, not even the constant energy required by a newborn. However, like all worthwhile endeavors, it will require practice and consistency. *Listen, Learn, Love* will dramatically improve your relationships in 30 days or less! I have seen this happen countless times as skeptics become believers.

In the beginning, practicing these skills may feel awkward and uncomfortable. That's okay. In fact, it's normal. They are new and unfamiliar. It's a bit like putting on a pair of stiff jeans. For the Boomer crowd, remember the jeans that stood up on their own before we washed, bleached, and conditioned them to death in the old days before acid and pre-washed jeans? For Millennials, these are jeans you line-dried and are a bit stiff or tight when you first put them on. Stiff jeans need to be worn and broken in.

Listen, Learn, Love are the same. Over time, with repeated use and wear, these skills will become more comfortable; like jeans, they will conform to your personal shape and style… or relationships. The more you use them, the more comfortable they become. Well-worn comfy jeans quickly become your go-to wardrobe staple. So go ahead and put on these skills; practice them as often as you can until they become second nature and are your go-to skills for building strong and satisfying relationships.

As you practice *Listen, Learn, Love* in your relationships, you will get more comfortable using these skills. Your relationships will improve because your loved ones, friends, and colleagues will see you investing time and energy in them... and that is one of the most universally meaningful gifts.

Imagine If...

- Your personal and professional relationships were the most enjoyable and satisfying parts of your life?
- Your day was full of conversations that flowed easily and led to greater intimacy with your spouse, deeper connection with your kids, synergy and productivity with your coworkers?
- You actually looked forward to family reunions because you had dealt with the elephants in the room and now spend time together making memories?
- You enjoying authentic and meaningful friendships where you felt known and appreciated?

Would you be willing to invest time and effort to experience these kinds of improvements in your relationships? Well, now you have the skills to make it happen. You can begin to create genuine, satisfying, and enjoyable relationships.

Listen, Learn Them, Love Well. Three simple, elegant, effective skills that can have huge impact!

Use them, practice, mess up, and try again. Dare greatly. Practice some more. Reread the book; review your notes. Try again. Celebrate every victory! Every improvement in your relationships, no matter how small, is a step in the right direction. Be patient with yourself and others. Jump scared. Don't give up.

Practice, practice, practice.

Start a *Listen, Learn, Love* movement in your life and watch your relationships improve!!

> *"I am convinced that material things can contribute a lot to making one's life pleasant, but basically, if you do not have very good friends and relatives who matter to you, life will be really empty and sad and material things cease to be important."*
> —David Rockefeller

Practicing *Listen, Learn, Love*

1. How is your relationship with your avatar(s)? As you have taken them and your relationship through each of these actions steps, are you more hopeful? Can you *see* improvement? Look at some of your notes and make a list of a few personal action steps specific to your relationships.

2. Review the practice exercises at the end of each chapter and do the ones you skipped.

3. Update your sticky notes for each skill and favorite tips. Go back through your dog-eared pages, highlights, and notes. This is "stuff" for your sticky notes. Make three or four copies of each one—Then put them up on your mirror, fridge, TV and/or dashboard to remind you to practice.

This may sound silly, but it really does work! When you see your *Listen, Learn, Love* notes (or the symbols if you are seeking subtlety), it will jog your memory, and remind you to use the skills.

I have one in my kitchen and at my desk: *Pause.* This helps me remember to slow my brain down. I have another on my bathroom mirror: *Don't explain—listen first.* My inner lawyer is on retainer, and I need this reminder daily. Life is busy, our world is noisy, and our brains are packed... A reminder to *Listen, Learn, Love* the people in your life could make the difference between actually doing it instead of just wanting to.

4. Connect with me and share at least one story from your journey on the *Listen, Learn, Love* Community page at *www.ListenLearnLoveCommunity.com/stories.*

Also, would you do me a favor? Post one question, on the Community page, about using these skills in your relationships. It will help me know what additional things to write about in *Listen, Learn, Love* blog posts, a workbook, or even the next edition.

***ListenLearnLoveCommunity.com* is there for you.**

Come join our community! It's important to know you're not in this alone. I would love to hear about moments of connection, understanding, increased ease, or how practicing and implementing these skills impacted your relationships. And, if you feel you need more time, tools, help, or encouragement, our *Listen, Learn, Love* Community is there to support and encourage you on your journey.

Remember, we're all in this together. I can't wait to connect and hear your stories!

Join us! *ListenLearnLoveCommunity.com* is there for you. It's important to know you don't have to do this *relationship stuff* alone. That is the whole point—building meaningful connections and engaging in relationships. In today's digital world, virtual relationships *can* be encouraging and genuine. *Listen, Learn, Love* Community is committed to creating a meaningful community offering support, resources, and connections. We can share success stories, post questions, and grow together. And when you join I have a little gift for you, just to say *Thanks.*

Go to: *ListenLearnLoveCommunity.com* to join, share your stories, and connect with our community!

Acknowledgments

At the end of a movie, the music soars, the story ends, and the credits roll. While many folks are anxious to leave, I always stay till the bitter end, until all the names of all the people who helped make the movie are recognized. With keen interest, I watch as the names scroll by—main characters, the stars, give way to the supporting actors, and then the team of unknowns—the "backbone" of the movie, without whom it would be incomplete, unfinished, and less amazing. Sitting in the theater as the movie credits roll, I look for the names of the best boy, the gaffer, the key grip, even the "second assistant to the coordinator of the second team," thinking they should be recognized... They are someone's son, daughter, friend, sister, brother, dad or mom. So, I stay and I watch, reading as many names as possible as they fly by, pausing in acute awareness that, while unknown to most of us, they made essential contributions to the movie. Stay and watch sometime. It is fascinating to see the number of people required for success in any worthwhile venture.

If I tried to individually recognize and thank all the people who contributed to my story and the success of my adventure called life, this book would grow to the size of *War and Peace*. The multitudes of relationships behind the message of this book are impossible to name in these few pages. They are, however, written on my heart as each of you had a hand in shaping my life and these words.

Friends, ministry partners, colleagues, mentors, teachers, fellow sojourners... Thank you for sharing a bit of your life with me and for leaving your imprint on mine. I am forever grateful.

To all my clients: I am honored you chose to entrust me with your story, hopes, fears, relationships, and struggles. Your courage inspires me. It is my privilege to work with you. Together we grow.

There are, however, a few people I must thank personally...

David Dunham, my publisher: God smiled on me the day you read my manuscript and decided to take a chance on me! Your belief, attention, and care for me and this project made the process delightful. I pray God rewards your leap of faith. Cheers and gratitude to *Joel Dunham, Crystal Flores*, and the Dunham Books team. Your help and support were invaluable!

Special thanks to my editors, *Sissi Haner* and *Ann Dietrich*, whose expertise saved my readers from run-on sentences and awkward paragraphs, and made my message easier to read.

Andy Andrews, what a thrill to have an endorsement from one of my favorite authors. The wisdom in your books has impacted my life immensely. Thank you. And *Robert D. Smith*, I am grateful for your support and encouragement. To both of you, I am honored by your willingness to invest your time to bless a first-time author. This speaks volumes about your love of your craft and the people who venture down the writer's road.

Carrie Wilkerson, a generous and authentic mentor, who introduced me to the fascinating world of online business. You're a bright light of hope and an example of what is possible if we follow our dreams with grit, commitment, and a whole lot of heart. Thank you for investing and believing in me.

Karen Anderson, my trusted friend and wise guide—from when I was a young wife and mom to an excited and anxious first-time author—your honesty, humor, and love bless me. Your expertise, gift with words, and fingerprints are all over this book... Words can't express my gratitude.

Jim Palmer, my business coach: Thank you for your wise counsel, brilliant advice, and boundless belief in me and what I have to offer the world. Without your coaching and direction, this book might still be stuck in my head or on my hard drive. Thank you for holding me to a standard of excellence in business growth and success. A shout-out of gratitude to our amazing, supportive, and collaborative Mastermind group! It's a privilege to be part of your team and have you as part of mine.

Aleta & Mark, Amber, Debbie & Bill, Gamble & Jeff, Tina & Mark and your families: Your friendship on the journey has blessed, challenged, comforted, and sustained me and my family. Thank you! Two small words for a whole lot of gratitude.

To my prayer team, gratitude overflows for your willingness to walk with me, covering me and my ministry and work in prayer. I draw joy, comfort, and strength knowing together we are trusting and believing God will use this little book to bless others and draw them to a deeper relationship with Him.

Julie Burge, treasured friend, prayer warrior, speaker of truth, giver of grace. Thank you for teaching me to dream big and for cheering me on. Sharing laughter, tears, hopes, fears… just getting to *do life* with you is one of God's sweetest gifts to me! (Mark and your kiddos are a great part of the package deal!)

To all the Millers: Thank you for being a faith-filled family of entrepreneurs who view your business as ministry. After my faith, marrying John, your son and brother, was the best thing that ever happened to me.

Annie, Matt, Sam, Alex & Madison, family is not only a matter of blood, but of loving and being loved… grateful you are part of our family and in for the long haul.

Margie, Steph, Mike, and Shelly, my siblings: Hathaway Drive, Dad's lab at GW, Crockett Lane, John's shop, Presby Hospital, Minnesota Christmases… a mosaic of memories. Your loyalty and love makes me proud to be an Albert. (Dad, I miss you, and I can't wait to see you in Heaven.)

Mom: You are the wisest person I know. Your example of grace, resilience, and perseverance has taught me more about life and love than I can ever express. Thank you for speaking words of hope and belief to me, for telling me to "mortgage your faith" when mine was failing. What a gift to call you my mom and my friend.

Kate, Emily, and Zack: Being your mom is the most rewarding part of my life. You are my "why." Each of you, in your own way, has taught me that "life IS art," which also means you got the mess as well as the beauty since moms learn as we go. I'm sorry it was hard sometimes. I treasure your grace and patience... and the memories of laughter, movies and popcorn, reading, dinner conversations, soccer fields, crafts, projects, more conversations, and Surfside Beach. My heart swells with love, awe, and pride watching you grow into wise, giving, and loving adults. And *Scot*, thank you for loving Kate and becoming part of our family. Please keep telling everyone we are perfectly normal!

John, my North Star, best friend, shelter, and champion... You see me, know me... and love me so. I am blessed beyond words—which is saying a lot! Though God has given us much to bear, with you the journey is rich. You are my favorite. Your steadfast faith, servant heart, and unwavering belief are an anchor for our family and keep me sane. "I love us!"

And to my Indescribable God: being Yours is all that really matters... but I'm thankful for Your abundant blessings too.

I am awed and grateful You redeemed this winsome girl, and humbled that You've taken the broken pieces of my story and used them to draw others to You. Most of all, Thank You for loving me and delighting in me. *Solo de Gloria.*

About the Author

Susie Albert Miller, MA, MDiv is The *Better* Relationship Coach™. As a therapist and coach for the last 20+ years, Susie's passion is to help people keep from settling for mediocre relationships with those they love and, through the process, help them learn to love God, and even themselves, better. Susie helps people reduce stress, communicate effectively, and grow deeper in their faith by creating *better* relationships through tried and true methods for long-lasting results. Susie's personal life has often read like a Shakespearean tragedy but she's known for her outlook on life as a *"possibilitarian!"*

Over the years, Susie has helped countless men, women, and couples improve communication, increase intimacy, and create meaningful and enjoyable relationships. Susie is particularly passionate about equipping women to grow deeper in their faith, increase their self-confidence, and live in freedom. She believes in the power of God to change us and our relationships.

Although Susie holds a Masters in Counseling and a Masters of Divinity, she credits the "school of life" for her greatest learning. As a sought-after retreat and event speaker, Susie weaves stories, humor, and hope in her messages. She has been described as "dynamic, creative, engaging, and motivating—an electrical storm and infusion of energy."

Susie believes that messy can be good, as most of us learn more through making mistakes and needing second chances rather than taking the safe and tidy way. She believes grace is essential, because we are all a work in progress... and grace makes us kinder to ourselves and others.

Susie is married to her best friend, John, a serial entrepreneur. They have been married for 31 years and have three adult children, who bring them joy, laughter and lots of love—as well as more than a few wrinkles. She loves dark chocolate, good books, and lingering conversations.

Want to connect with Susie, The *Better* Relationship Coach? Go to *SusieMiller.com* and find out how to book her for your next event, read her blog, or connect with her on Facebook, Twitter, or Instagram (@susiemiller5). Susie loves meeting and connecting with people so make sure you stop by *SusieMiller.com* and say hello!